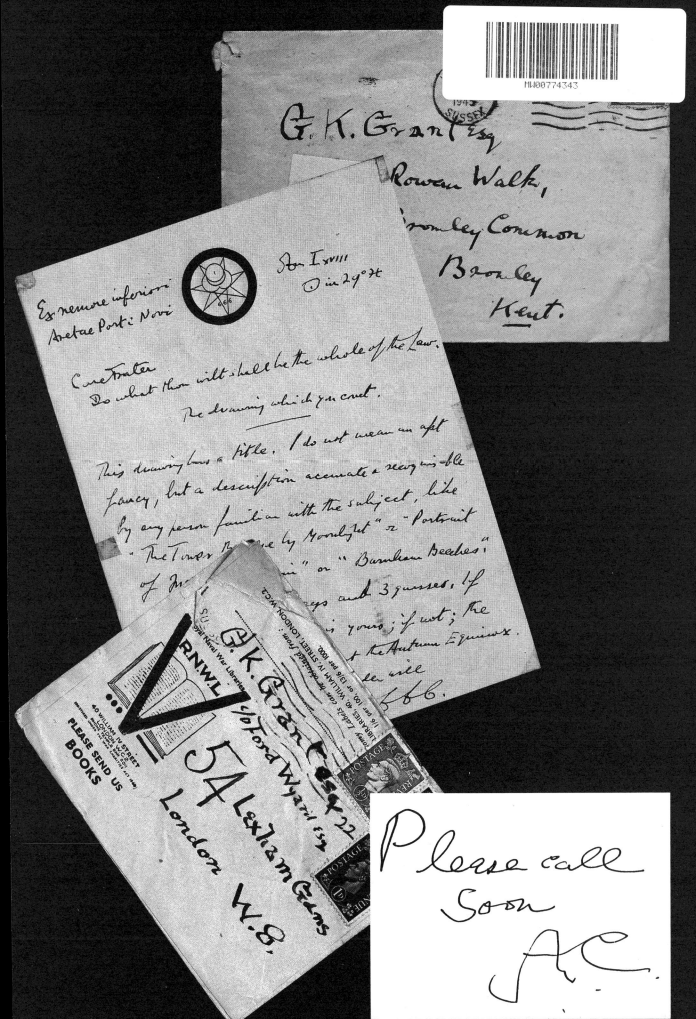

Envelope (top):

G.K. Grant Esq

Rowan Walk,

Bromley Common

Bromley

Kent.

[postmark: 1943 SUSSEX]

Letter:

An Lxviii
☉ in 29° ♓

Ex nemore inferiori
Aretae Porti Novi

Care Frater

Do what thou wilt shall be the whole of the Law.

Re drawing which you covet.

_____

This drawing has a title. I do not mean an apt fancy, but a description accurate & recognisable by any person familiar with the subject, like "The Tower Bridge by Moonlight" or "Portrait of _____" or "Burnham Beeches" ...... ss and 3 guineas. If ...... is yours; if not; the ...... the Autumn Equinox. ...... ee will

𝔄.𝔄.

Envelope (lower):

G.K. Grant Esq
c/o Lord Wyard 22
54 Lexham Gdns
London
W.8.

Card (bottom right):

Please call
soon

A.C.

REMEMBERING
ALEISTER CROWLEY

BY

KENNETH GRANT

SKOOB BOOKS PUBLISHING
LONDON

Copyright © Kenneth and Steffi Grant 1991
Series editor; Christopher Johnson

Published by
SKOOB BOOKS PUBLISHING LTD
Skoob esoterica series
11a-17 Sicilian Avenue
Southampton Row
London WC1A 2QH

ISBN 1 871438 22 5

Printed by Hillman Printers (Frome) Ltd

To
the memory of
DAVID CURWEN

ILLUSTRATIONS

INTRODUCTION

A few months before World War II, at the age of fifteen, I chanced upon a book in the Charing Cross Road entitled *Magick in Theory and Practice*, by Aleister Crowley. It led to my reading as many of Crowley's writings as I could lay hands on. They were difficult to come by, and expensive.

My main interest was (and still is) in Oriental Mysticism. When I volunteered for the army, at the age of eighteen, it was with the expectation of being sent to India where I had hopes of finding a guru. But the gods decided otherwise. Within eighteen months of joining, my health broke down and I was discharged.

After convalescence, I struck up a correspondence with Crowley. He had recently published, from 93 Jermyn Street, his sumptuous volume on the Tarot, and was engaged on a new work which he called *Aleister Explains Everything*. I mention the fact because I was to take down at his dictation some of its contents. This proved of salutary value to me as it provided a unique opportunity for first-hand discussion on matters that concerned both of us. The book was published, long after his death, as *Magick Without Tears*.

Crowley was almost, but not quite, at the end of the road. His mind remained keen and alert; but ill-health, old age and the air-raids had driven him from London. He was staying at the Bell Inn, in Buckinghamshire, when I first met him in 1944.

Before and after my stay with him at the guest-house in Hastings, where he finally settled, we exchanged letters. I do not think many of mine survived, but some of Crowley's did, and I have often been urged to publish them. I well remember awaiting the arrival of the envelopes bearing the cartouche of Ankh-af-na-Khonsu with which he usually sealed them in blood-red or grey-blue wax. With few exceptions the letters were written in his own sharp hand.

I have provided comments in order to give glimpses of a little recorded period of Crowley's life. Crowley had not entirely pulled out of his London apartment in Jermyn Street, and, inevitably, I was enlisted to assist in the tiresome process of extracting from a long-suffering and unsympathetic landlady his remaining possessions.

Despite my dismal failure to satisfy the Master's unremitting demands, this period was for me richly rewarding. Personal association with Crowley was a profound initiation if one could dive beneath the surface and seize the luminous prize. I was sometimes able to do this; but I was unable ever to acquire a practical approach to mundane affairs, a lack which so exasperated Crowley.

I am acutely aware of my failure adequately to portray a relationship which was, from the start, unequal in so many ways. He was sixty-nine, and replete with worldly experience; I was twenty, with hardly any.

I have occasionally drawn upon Crowley's unpublished diaries, and other correspondence, in order to elucidate specific references in the letters, and in so doing I have to thank Crowley's literary executor. For the design of this book - indeed, for its appearance - I am grateful to my wife, Steffi.

Sekhet

Shall it be claws or paws to-day,
Jehane, your lover-lion play?
Sweetness of torment bring completeness
To love, or torment sharpen sweetness?

Breast against bosom, shall I feel
The lure of velvet or of steel?
Will it be fire or water flies
From the wild opal of your eyes?

Will you express your spirit-stress
By laughter or by holiness?
I care not - either serves our play -
If it be claws or paws to-day.

Aleister Crowley

Sekhet.

Shall it be claws or paws to-day,
Jehane, your lover-lion play?
Sweetness of torment bring completeness
To love, or torment sharpen sweetness?

Breast against bosom, shall it feel
The lure of velvet or of steel?
Will it be fire or water flies
From the wild opal of your eyes?

Will you express your spirit-stress
By laughter or by holiness?
I care not — either serves our play —
If it be claws or paws to-day.

Aleister Crowley

I work on gold, and gold must be cleansed with acid.
~ Crowley, in *Magick Without Tears*

G.K. Grant, Esq.,

The Bell Inn
Aston Clinton,
Bucks.
November 17th, 1944.

Dear Sir,

Do what thou wilt shall be the whole of the Law.

I got your letter this morning and was very interested in what you have to say. I am the head of certain organisations which I think might be of service to you. You mention that you have a number of my works, but you do not specify which. I should like to know this in case there are certain gaps which I might be able to fill. In particular, do you possess my prize work, The Book of Thoth? I am sending you a prospectus, but I am obliged to ask you to send me the cost of it, as I have got into trouble with the Ministry of Supply for distributing them free of charge. I do not think they are within their rights for various technical reasons with which I will not trouble you. But at least we may as well keep on the safe side. This book should be of great value to you as it sums up practically the whole of my knowledge in the particular study with which it deals.

Love is the law, love under will.

Yours sincerely,

Aleister Crowley

pp.J.T. {Janet Taylor}.

{In A.C's hand:} Did you get this? A.C.

{In A.C's hand referring to an enclosed note by GPO concerning Prospectus which had been found loose in P.O.}: Sorry! It was my Super-secretary. A.C.

I first wrote to Crowley in early November at the Jermyn Street address given in *The Book of Thoth*. I had seen a copy in an 'occult' book shop in Museum Street. The proprietor, Michael Houghton, had persistently refrained from disclosing Crowley's address, hinting at possible karmic consequences resulting from my meeting him. I learned later that Houghton had earmarked me for his own organization, The Order of Hidden Masters, and was displeased with my growing interest in Crowley and his work. Even so, he tried to sell me everything by Crowley that he acquired in ways that occasionally aroused Crowley's suspicions.

November 18th is a red-letter day in the Crowley mythos, being the date of his initiation, in 1898, into The Hermetic Order of the Golden Dawn. He replied to my letter on the 17th., not doubting that it would reach me the following day. But a war was on and the postal services were already foreshadowing their present-day level of inefficiency. Also, the Ministry of Supply had instituted enquiries concerning the paper used for the prospectus of *The Book of Thoth* which, by war-time standards, seemed suspiciously lavish. Crowley had been visited by an official on October 30th., 1944: "...man from Ministry of Supply. God! Accepted hospitality; asked me to lunch; didn't warn me before questioning. He admitted that there had been a complaint (Gestapo-wise) so they were officially obliged to enquire", Crowley had noted in his diary.

Crowley's secretary had held back the letter to enclose the prospectus, so the letter would in any case have been delayed.

Bell Inn   {Aylesbury 27 Nov 44}
Aston Clinton   Nov 27 '44 e.v.
Bucks

Dear Sir

Do what thou wilt shall be the whole of the Law.

(N.B. Change not even style of any letter: e.g. caps for l.c. Injunction thrice repeated in AL.)

Yours of 26th duly to hand with cheque: receipt herewith enclosed. The books will go off to-morrow, when I have some one to undertake the 8-mile pilgrimage to the P.O.

You are really very lucky - or deserving - to have so many. Of course there are ever so many more: I wish I had copies myself of I don't even know how many there ought to be. It is a weird story.

Liber Aleph. There seems to be a curse on this book. It has been ready for the Press ever since 1919 e.v. and always something turns up to prevent the printing. Now, of course, there is less hope than ever. The only solution is to buy a printer, or a share in one big enough to ensure priority. Half a dozen other books, too, all most important and urgent, and I'm helpless. You will find several chapters of Liber א [1] e.g., pp 122-128. It's maddening! It *is* such an exciting book!

Look here, I think I'll take a chance and get my one and only copy typed afresh, though I hate letting it out of my hands even for a day. Would you be willing to pay the typist's account, and let me have the two carbons - you taking the top copy, of course - for my pains? It would take about 3 weeks, at a guess, and should not cost more than £ 3.0.0. Anyhow, if it should come to more, I'll pay the excess.

———————————

I am sorry to say that there are no copies left of The Book of the Law. It will of course be reprinted at the first opportunity. There is, I believe, an American edition recently printed. You might apply to Mr. K.J. Germer 260 West 72nd. St New York City 23.N.Y. U.S.A.

———————————

There are some local printers at Ilford, I fancy. Perhaps you could persuade one to cram in a small job like this? If you could, you would indeed "make merit"!

Now with regard to your present position. If I am to assume responsibility, I ought to know a great deal. (1) Have you your horoscope? If so, please send me a copy - Chaldean form preferred. If not, the data: year, month, day & hour as exact as possible, of birth and place. (2) It is useless for me to advise a course which is impossible; so I want to know something of your family [2], education, occupation, resources &c &c. Are you married? Any children? I'm not being inquisitive; I only want to be able to judge the sort of things that you can do, and that suit you. You'll understand, I'm sure.

I well know how you feel about the practical side of things: (By the way, are you a Freemason?).

It is *very* welcome to hear that I am lucid. For years nearly everybody has been kicking me for being obscure. In fact, my new book consists of a series of letters, answering *colloquially* every kind of question that would occur to any intelligent person. About 70 ready, so far; it will probably run to 100 —— Hum —— Ha —— ? —— ? {A reference to *Aleister Explains Everything*, posthumously published as *Magic Without Tears*.}

The more I think things over, the more I feel that the best plan would be for you to run out here & lunch with me. (Marylebone to Aylesbury 9.45 A.M. then 'bus drops you at the door. Longish journey - you could get a room for the night except at week-ends.)

I will send you details of O.T.O. and more about the new book in the meanwhile.

Love is the law, love under will.

Yours sincerely,

Aleister Crowley.

{included in the letter, a receipt:}

93 Jermyn St
S.W.1.

Nov 27
'44 e.v.

Recd of G.K.Grant Esq
     by cheque
the sum of Ten Guineas £ 10.10.0
     for one copy of The Equinox Vol III No 5.
        (The Book of Thoth)

{A.C.'s signature appears over a 2[d] stamp.}

[1]{Aleph}

[2]{note in A.C's hand}: It's a large clan, I know; but do you know Gregor Fergus Grant, of the Customs Fund, or - ? my cousin. A.C.

Crowley was a stickler for detail, especially when it came to *The Book of the Law*. The Book, which was transmitted to him in Cairo in 1904 by a discarnate Intelligence named Aiwass was the foundation of his work. It was first published in The Equinox vol. I, No. 7, {1912}.

Liber Aleph, subtitled *The Book of Wisdom or Folly*, was completed in 1918 when Crowley was in the U.S.A. Written originally for his 'magical son', Frater Achad{Charles Stansfeld Jones, 1886-1950}, it languished in manuscript until Karl Germer published it in the U.S., in 1961. Pages 122-128 of *The Book of Thoth* {1944}. contain extracts from *Liber Aleph*.

When Crowley eventually set up my horoscope, he summed it up in his diary on January 4th, 1945: "Read Grant's horror {sic}; much better than I thought at first; but most unusual." {See illustration facing page}

The Bell Inn
Aston Clinton,
Bucks
Dec 2. {1944}

Dear Mr Grant
    Do what thou wilt shall be the whole of the Law
                (capital L for Law)
Yours of Nov 28 & ☾ ☍ ☉ duly to hand: thanks.

I am very glad that you are pleased with the book: you should find it a quite encyclopaedic Alphabet on which to base your Magical Thinking.

It is best always to make cheques payable to me personally, and sent to the address where I am staying at the time. Jermyn St might fail to forward them.

You write as if you had already the particulars of the O.T.O., but I do not remember sending them. It is a typescript of some 40 pages. If you have not got them, let me know, and I will send by return post.

I can't find a copy of my first letter to you, if I ever wrote one - memory plays me false at times. But I had *intended* to ask many questions: have you a horoscope, or will you send me the data? Are you a Freemason? Your circumstances, family, education, occupation, etc. I am not being inquisitive; but there are many things I must know if I am to advise you intelligently.

Love is the law, love under will
Yours sincerely 666.

P.S. re Lunch

Sunday is quite all right for me, but this is 4 miles from Aylesbury, and there are no 'buses on Sunday before 1. You can get a taxi, but I must know a day or so beforehand.

The Manchester Express (9.45 A.M. or near it) reaches Aylesbury about 11 after only 2 halts. 1st class carriages & all comforts. The slow trains are pre-Boer war, when not pre-Crimean!

Getting back is easier; Express passes at 6.5 P.M. or near it. Also later trains, though not so quick or so good.

You write, though, as if you have a car; if so, splendid; you keep N. of London.
    A.C.

Kenneth Grant   8.00 A.M. May 23, '24

S.T. 4.3.54.17
      4
   0.3.54.17

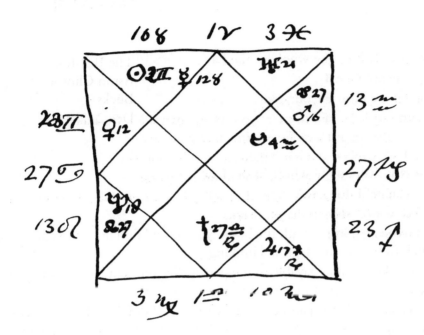

16 ♉   1 ♈   3 ♓

☉ 2 ♊   ☿ 12 ♉
                    ♃ ⛢ 24
28 ♊   ♇ 27 ♐
♀ 12   ♂ 16
                 13 ♏
27 ♋   ♅ 4 ♒
                 27 ♑
13 ♌
♃ 18   ☊ 27
♄ 27 ♎   27 ♑
      ♄ 27 ♎   23 ♐
      24 17 ♐
3 ♍   1 ♎   10 ♏

☽ △ ☉ ⚹
♇ △ ♃ ☌ ♅ ☍ ♂
♀ △ ♂ ⚹ ☿ ☍ □ ♃

♄ exalted
♃ lord

(above) Horoscope by Crowley,
(right) Dedication in *Equinox of the Gods*

THE EQUINOX
OF THE GODS

Frater ... 400

Cum benedictione summa
τοῦ ... 666

An I☉in 0°0'0" ♈

Bell Inn
Aston Clinton
Bucks.
Dec 7 [1944]

Dear Mr Grant

Do what thou wilt shall be the whole of the Law.

Many thanks for yours of Dec 4.

The particulars so far are most encouraging.

I am arranging with our local taxi to meet you; so on arrival ask for Baker. In my turn, I will mention your name, so as to avoid any smash & grab tactics.

I will keep the O.T.O. papers, and hand them to you on Sunday.

Do get your birth date accurate, especially the hour, if possible.

I don't know how late the trains run; here they tell you a dozen different stories. Best to ask personally at the station when you get there.

Love is the law, love under will.

Till Sunday, then,

Sincerely

Aleister Crowley

Sunday the 10th December 1944, a bleak and snowy day, was the date of my first meeting with the master. His diary entry reads:

"Sun 10. Kieh - 40. Grant arrived; managed to get taxi after all. Got his rising sign right. Cancer {sign for}. Aet 20. Eheu! fugaces labuntur omni {Alas , the fleeting years glide by!} Would I were at Nefta, and 25! Yî symbol for him Liu XIX, Pisces Fire {signs for}.

H.A. dashed in!!! Whole bloody day enquiring, instructing, confirming K.T.L. ad nauseam. Oh so blasted tired! But very happy."

H.A. was Frater Hymenaeus Alpha - Grady McMurtry - 1918–1985, an American follower of Crowley. At the time of our meeting he was a lieutenant in the U.S. army, and stationed in Germany. He was devoted to Crowley and, when on leave, he grabbed every opportunity to see him. His visits sometimes induced in Crowley physical exhaustion to the point of prostration, as noted in Crowley's diary for 1945. While speaking to me, on one occasion, McMurtry referred repeatedly to "the Master here", until Crowley, exasperated, began searching the room in an attempt to find Him. Crowley appeared embarrassed when anyone referred to him, in his presence, by any of the honorifics which he freely lavished on himself – in print.

Bell Inn
Aston Clinton
Bucks

Dec 18 {1944}

Care Frater

   Do what thou wilt shall be the whole of the Law.

Yours of Dec 13th. Delay in reply due to invasion: wave upon wave!

I was indeed sorry that our F∴ H.A. should have dropped on us so unexpectedly.

Do make up for it by coming out here again – any day from Saturday next will do, provided you telephone the day before.

1924. You could probably get the data by telephoning an Astrological Journal or some pro{fessional} like Naylor. Mention my name. All you need is the position of the 9 planets and Caput Draconis at noon on the day of your birth. Jot them down, and forward. *Show resource.*

O.T.O. Eqx.III.1. printed as in N.Y. {New York} so I put in both currencies.

The A∴A∴ is for personal initiation; O.T.O. is for groups, & not nearly as important.

Never mind *reading* History; it is for you to *write* it.

I hope your multigraph papers will be ready before Jan{uary} 1.

Get all ready in your mind as to what you want to ask me; make notes; check off as I answer.

Love is the law, love under will.

Fraternally yours

666

No Scarlet Button?

Crowley's copy of *The Equinox*, vol. III, number 1 {the 'Blue' Equinox} was bound in brown buckram and bore upon its front cover the sunblaze symbol of the A∴A∴, enclosing the Eye within the Triangle associated with the Order of the Illuminati, an historic manifestation of the O.T.O., founded by Adam Weishaupt {1748-1830}. While at "Netherwood" I spent many an evening, after Crowley had retired for the night, poring over this massive volume which had been published in 1919. It was by dint of classing it as a periodical, and describing it as an instalment of *The Equinox* series, that Crowley was able to circumvent war-time restrictions and bring out his magnificent volume on the Tarot many years later.

The multigraph papers comprised *Liber II*, 'The Manifesto of the O.T.O.'. *The Scarlet Button*: the title of a novel which Crowley was anxious to procure; I forget why.

Bell Inn
Aston Clinton
Bucks

Dec 22 {1944}

Care Frater,

Do what thou wilt shall be the whole of the Law.

[Care Frater, or, to an $8° = 3^{\square}$, Care Magister, is the 'correct' way to begin; "Yours fraternally" (if he is in the Order) to finish.]

Many thanks for yours of 18th; but "about Thursday" - is that the 21st or 28th?

"Hectic" = continuous. Dean Inge gave a further instance of his ignorance by objecting to young people saying "We had a hectic time" or the like. They were precisely correct.

I will advise about the Sigil when I have set up your horoscope.

Your letter arrived on the day of the Solstice; thanks for the good wishes. "The same to you, only louder!"

Love is the law, love under will.

Yours sincerely & fraternally

666

P.S. This is important for me to know at once: are your parents in sympathy with your interest in these matters which concern us?

Any hope of seeing you this week-end or next?

666.

{The square brackets, first paragraph, are Crowley's.}

The instructions as to correct mode of address I duly followed in all my further letters to Crowley. The reader should consult *Magick*, pages 327-328 for a full explanation of the A∴A∴ Grade System, and the titles of the grades.

The reference to the sigil was elicited by letter-headings on my note paper in the form of my personal seal. Before commenting on it, Crowley wanted to set up my horoscope.

TEL: Aston Clinton 4.   [1 P.M, 4 onward P.M. are the
                                         sure hours.]

Bell Inn
Aston Clinton
Bucks   Dec 23. 1944
                                                   ☉ in 18° ♑

Care Frater
    Do what thou wilt shall be the whole of the Law.
Your two letters, dated between Feb 19 and March 21, seem to have taken a long time to
arrive! Very welcome.
Your usual luck still attends you. There were only 2 copies {Book of Thoth} left till – when
the binder finishes the next batch. It is not luck that your copy is bound in $^1/_2$ not $^1/_4$
Morocco; any one who buys two or more copies gets one of them like that. But it *is* luck
that you get such an early copy; they sent me an assorted lot without looking! Idiots! Still,
you profit. It is on the way. I thought you would like me to inscribe it; so I did.
Many thanks for the 99 that safely lie in the shelter of the fold. The one that's lost on the
hills away Far off from the gates of gold Away on the mountains wild and bare Away from
the tender shepherd's care can bloody well stay there.
The A∴A∴ & O.T.O. are quite asynartete, save that the latter body has accepted the Law
of Thelema. "One Star in Sight" tells all about A∴A∴ & the typescripts I sent you (didn't
I?) all about O.T.O. I can't understand your confusing them.
Well — when we meet.
Love is the law, love under will.
F∴ly {Fraternally}   ⚔   Baphomet X° 33° 90° 96°

{Above letter contained}:
Bell Inn Aston Clinton Bucks
Dec 23, '44 e.v.
Received from G.K.Grant Esq. on behalf of the Grand Treasurer General of the O.T.O.
the sum of {illegible} £ 10.10.0. Aleister Crowley {over postage stamp}.

In his inscription in my copy of *The Book of Thoth* {see illustration}, Crowley uses
my personal magical sigil.

'One Star in Sight': an essay written by Crowley at the Abbey of Thelema, Cefalù,
Sicily, in 1921. It first appeared in *Magick in Theory and Practice*, Lecram Press,
Paris, 1929.

'Baphomet' was Crowley's magical name, or title, as Outer Head of the Order
{O.H.O.}, i.e. of the *Ordo Templi Orientis* {O.T.O.}. It was the name of the
God of the Knights Templar Order and was generally considered to have been

Dedications in *Orpheus* and
the *Book of Thoth*

Aleister Crowley

Library Copy.

[dedication handwritten]

into what remains is
the Memory of one of the most
Pleasant Afternoons
that I remember

Jan 4 1945 e.v.

Aleister Crowley

To ⚛

this copy № 33
with the wish that he may soon be able
to write 33° after his name

Baphomet
X° 33° 90° p 5°

goat-headed. Like the zoötype of the god Set, in Egypt, the entity has not been accurately identified. The degrees following the name are,respectively, those of the Ancient and Accepted Scottish Rite of Masonry, and of the Egyptian Rites of Mizraim and Memphis, all of which degrees were claimed by Crowley.

The biblical allusion to the lost sheep remains lost to me after forty-five years.

The Bell Inn
Aston Clinton,
Bucks.
December 30th, 1944

Dear Mr.Grant,

Do what thou wilt shall be the whole of the law. {sic}

I am glad you will have a free day next week. Any day will suit me after Wednesday. Things here are in a most awful mess. Pipes frozen is the least of my troubles.

I will give you the £ 2 2 0d. on your arrival. Don't forget to remind me of that.

I was not at all sure about your poem. So far I can only see magnified words and no core, but this morning I am in no condition to judge anything.

I am glad to get Ephemeris. There is nothing worth reading in Lyndoe's book except the tables at the end which enable one to dispense with the actual Ephemeris for the years from 1860-1920 if one is doing only a rough figure.

Love is the law, love under will.

Aleister Crowley

pp. JT

Hoping to see you towards the end of next week.

{In A.C's hand, enclosed in letter on separate scrap}:

My question "Are your parents sympathetic?" is important, because, if you like the idea, it *might* be possible to fix up a full-time job. (You would have to learn shorthand & typing, of course). You would learn a lot & fit yourself for an official position in the Order in say 10 or 15 years' time 666.

The poem does not survive.

He begins making a move to form with me a working relationship. The P.S. is in his own hand, doubtless because he did not wish it to be read by his typist, whose redundancy his plans implied.

Bell Inn
Aston Clinton
Bucks

Jan 6 {1945}

Care Frater

Do what thou wilt shall be the whole of the Law.

Not only delightful, your visit {Jan 4}, but (I feel) most fruitful; the Yî King owed it to me, for the day's hexagram was "Great Havings", and all the other things were Income Tax demands, bills, and other items "in the red".

But the pleasure made me forget one matter of vast import; I want you to do a bit of Magical Shopping for me. This.

I need a Disk. It must be circular, and gold.

The ideal is a zecchino (sequin) issued by Pope Alexander VI; it represents the Miraculous Draught of Fishes. This is a well-known coin; there were two up at auction some 10 months ago, & I just missed them. If one should be available, it must be in "mint condition". You might telephone Spink's, the London Bullion Co, & a few other specialists in coins. If in vain, advertisement might do the trick.

Second string. Any Oriental gold coin or medal (e.g. a gold mohur). This also must be perfect & heavy & thick. An American "Double Eagle" might do. Preferably, no portrait. (I forget whether Double Eagles have them) a coin or medal, all Arabic characters, is perhaps the best bet.

Sorry to burden you, but ————

Love is the law, love under will.

Fraternally 666.

Crowley regularly consulted the *Yî King* {Legge's translation}. Hexagram XIV, 'Great Havings', was the omen he obtained on January 4th., 1945, the date of my second visit to him. He commemorated the occasion by inscribing for me a copy of the rare one-volume edition of his epic poem, *Orpheus*, published from Boleskine, Scotland, in 1905. {See illustration}

I went to Spink's {Art Dealers, Jewellers, Medalists, of St. James} and bought a gold mohur. I was unaware that it was to form the basis of a Magical Operation initiated by Crowley to facilitate our working together. The story of the mohur is quite involved. Crowley used gold disks or coins in connection with astral visions. On one occasion, I saw him slip something into his mouth before I closed my eyes at the outset of a test in the spirit-vision. That it was the mohur is confirmed by a diary-entry dated February 20th., 1946, in which Crowley described a similar test given to Frater Merlinus {Frederick Mellinger}, a member of the American branch of the O.T.O. At about the time of my own test, Crowley gave me a finger-ring of alloyed gold which consisted of the twelve zodiacal signs. After my departure from Hastings, I suffered severe nightmares - unusual for me

- and an alarming depletion of energy. I also noticed, one morning, that half the sign of Cancer {my rising sign} was missing from the ring. I recalled the story of the train-driver in Crowley's novel *Moonchild*, and decided to perform a little magick myself, after which I purified it by fire in an oven, and then consigned it to the river Roding in Essex {purification by water}, near to where I was living at the time.

In November, 1945, Crowley noted in his diary that his mohur was missing. He sent off to Spink's for a substitute. On November 8th, Spink's sent him "a zecchin issued by me in 1492 e.v.". That is to say, the zecchin or disk was struck by Pope Alexander VI, who Crowley claimed to have been in one of his former embodiments.

On March 11th., 1946, Crowley noted in his diary: "Nice old man came back to tend garden {i.e. the garden at 'Netherwood'} - and found my gold mohur!!!". This was the disk which I had originally obtained for him.

The Bell Inn
Aston Clinton,
Bucks.
January 10th, 1945

Care Frater,

Do what thou wilt shall be the whole of the law. {sic}

I have just got yours of the 8th January and hasten to answer it because from now on I shall not be able to reply to anything until I have got settled down in Hastings where I propose to transport myself today week.

I don't care what state "The Scarlet Button" is in as long as the copy is complete.

We can discuss the question of Pitman's later on.

I have no idea where you can get a Blue Equinox which is Vol.3, No. 1 and is bound in blue cloth. Hence the nickname.

As to the Goetia, the same applies though there is a little more hope because it was pirated in the U.S. by some thieving scoundrel. I think it was done photographically so it would be quite as good as the original edition except that it is a little smaller than the original, but I should not bother myself about it if I were you because it really does not matter. There is actually nothing whatever in the book that is worth reading to anyone as advanced as you are. The one interesting point about it was the "initiated interpretation" of ceremonial magic which gave a strictly rationalistic explanation of various thaumaturgical feats. For instance, by invoking some particular Demon you obtain the power to do this, that and the other. For example, to speak languages {un}known to you. This can be explained by supposing that the process of evocation stimulates that section of your brain which helps you to learn languages. The various other miracles can be explained in a similar quite simple way. Now then, you have got as much as you would have if you possessed the book and

studied it for 40 years. Don't expect to hear from me again until I have settled at Hastings.
Love is the law, love under will.
Aleister Crowley
pp. JT

Pitman's Secretarial College, Southampton Row, London.
Crowley's typist-of-the-moment evidently mistook 'invocation' for 'evocation',
an error of which Crowley would not have been guilty.
Crowley's comments on *The Goetia* were proved to be sound.

Bell   die ☽ ae {die lunae/day
                                                        of the moon, i.e. Monday
                                                        postmarked 16 Jan 1945.}

C∴F∴ {Care Frater}
93
Pleurisy being pleurisy, I can't answer letters.
Not bad – 99.2° {his temperature} for days, but intractable – till this last minute, when it
has gone back to normal 98.4°. Thank God!
And no one to help, bar very occasional & important things.
Your Pitman pit appals! Probably they teach you lots of commercial things quite useless for
our purpose. Surely private tuition would be easier. Consider your intelligence. All you
need is (a) the system (b) dodges (c) training your fingers to find the keys without looking
(d) practice.
But don't think of your "new job" as if it were a sitting bird; I shall have to shoot an oof-bird
myself in order to furnish you feathers to fly with!
Question   A: what will it cost you to live in ordinary decent comfort in a place like
Hastings? B: What would you need for pocket -money - clothes, smokes, drinks, κ.τ.λ
{etc}. C: Anything else you can think of.
I must know what it will cost me - rather, the O.T.O. then write and make sure I get it.
I feel sure that Ilford has some teacher quite adequate for evening tuition.
Very many thanks for Secret Glory {Arthur Machen}; best of his I've read. Criticism when
I'm strong enough.
Too tired to write more; hope adequate answer when Miss T{aylor} comes Wednesday.
93 $^{93}/_{93}$ F∴ly{Fraternally} 666.

The number 93 is of major importance in Crowley's system of magick. It is the
sum of the letters comprising the Greek words for Will {*thelema*}, and Love

{*agapé*}. For many other correspondences the reader should consult Crowley's works, particularly *Sepher Sephiroth* { *The Equinox*, vol. 1. No. 8.}

Shooting an oof-bird is tantamount to saying "when my ship comes home". The oof-bird was a fabulous creature, sometimes equated with the Arabian roc, and with the phoenix that appeared periodically, and which denoted a cycle of time.

Bell Inn   die ♄ {Saturday}

C∴F∴   {postmark: Aylesbury
                                                                             21 Jan 1945}

93

Thanks for yours of 18th. You mustn't tempt me to discuss Secret Glory; too much to say. This pleurisy is a joke, but on the "Punch" level. No pain, no dyspnoea beyond my normal ration, temperature never over a 100° & that goes down to normal or near it every night. Then in A.M. it's up again! Pure perversity.

The local witch doctor has given me the "newest" ju-ju, with the most fantastic precautions; he was obviously afraid to prescribe it! But I shall start tomorrow 8 A.M. if this fool thermometer keeps on jumping about.

I think both your estimates on the high side, unless you want to live *en prince*. Even in London there are quite decent boarding-houses at £ 2.2.0 The country is always cheaper. Don't lump clothes with smoke & drinks. You want 2 or 3 suits at not less than £ 16.16.0 then they last 10 years or more; and the *appearance* is worth money. Shoes you can get at £4 - £6. Shirts about £ 2.10.0. Really, one rule only; the dearest things are the cheapest. (I'm an expert, by the way, & can help a lot with advice and introductions.) Avoid cheap cigarettes as the very devil. Best is: pipe only, and *real* tobacco. One smokes less, & so saves in the long run; besides, you don't poison yourself, and you feel like a man. Drink: at your age, the less the better. Beer would be good if you could get it; but can you? I'll ask; I don't drink it myself. Bar cocktails; whiskey is good in *strict* moderation; but the proprietorial brands are mostly muck. "Black Label", "Haig", "Dimple", "Victoria Vat", and some of the special merchants like Hedges & Butler. But 9 times in 10 it is best to say no.

At present wine is not to be bought.

I am working out a plan that may help you. Also, there are ways of dodging taxes; I know some.

I got the smokes [1], thanks. What do I owe you?

93 ⁹³/₉₃ Hoping to move ♃ or ♀ next {Thursday or Friday}. F∴ly 666.

[1] {Weinsberg Special (Burlington Arcade)}

The first allusion to a scheme that would enable us to work together when he moved to Hastings. On January 20th {1945}, Crowley wrote to his life-long friend, the novelist Louis Marlow {Louis Wilkinson}: "...I am making arrangements for the future. You are the natural man for my literary executor...I have just found an ideal assistant literary executor, and am starting to train him..." And a few days later, January 27th., Crowley wrote again to Wilkinson: "there is a youth called Kenneth Grant, not quite 21, who has been collecting and studying me for the last three years. I am trying to get him to look after me and my work. He must learn shorthand and typing; but we can start at once (more or less) once I get to Hastings, provided we can put finance on a sound basis. Brief: a definite gift from the Gods. An ideal person to do all the hard work under your direction."

Crowley's favourite brand of cigarettes - at this time - was Weinsberg Special. They were bland and highly aromatic, and were obtainable in the Burlington Arcade, Piccadilly.

Bell Inn   die ☽ ae
                                                                 {Monday}
                                                                 {23 Jan 1945}

C∴F∴
    93
Provided that I can get a car, and have no further trouble from the Himalayas, and that the weather is not impossible, I shall shift ♃ or ♀ {Thursday or Friday} to
              c/o Vernon Symonds Esq
              Netherweed {sic}
              The Ridge
              Hastings
It has struck me that it might help you to get a move on if you took a job similar to your own in a local bookseller's. They are probably screaming for help.
Would enable you to put in a lot of spare time usefully, and you could help me by taking letters in longhand while you learn. And by sorting out papers: this needs doing very badly indeed. You would also get the hang of things & save time later on. Would you agree to such a plan if I could fix it? If so, send me details so that I know what to say to the blokes. There is said to be a cottage to let, part of the hotel; we might possibly find that useful. Know nothing about it; mention it as part of the Magical Formula of the whole Opus.

If, by some miracle, the way were clear, how soon could you start? Important for me to know this.
Excuse scrappiness; I've written this at odd minutes when I thought of something.
93 $^{93}/_{93}$ F∴ly 666.
P.S. {on envelope:} "Provided that", No 1, seems *very* difficult.
P.P.S. A glimmer shows on the horizon

"Trouble from the Himalayas", refers to Crowley's asthma, contracted during his Himalayan expedition {see *The Confessions*}. This was the 'storm fiend' which thereafter attacked him periodically and for which, originally, he was prescribed heroin, before its adverse side-effects became known.

On receipt of this letter, I thought I understood Crowley's request for the gold disk; it was to help him acquire for our use the cottage in the grounds of 'Netherwood'. The use of a disk or coin in connection with magick is traditional. There is a good example of such use in Crowley's novel *Moonchild*. The coin I intended buying at Spink's had been struck by Awadh Ghazi-ud-Din Haidar, in A.H. 1236.

> The Bell Inn
> Aston Clinton, Bucks.
> January 24th, 1945

Care Frater,

I got your letter this morning with great pleasure. Since I wrote yesterday the glimmer of light has become what appears to be a very steady spark, though the details are still very complicated. I cannot go by car, I have to go by ambulance and they won't stop for half an hour on the way to let me do my business in Oxford. I do not quite know how they figure this out so that it is a saving of petrol. I am quite at the mercy of the ambulance as to when they can take me and this complicates things for me in another way which is really too awful to contemplate. Really all this business does work out to be a training in ingenuity if in nothing else.

Many thanks and congratulations and compliments on finding the Mohur. I should want to know, however, the measurements and the weight, also whether it is badly rubbed. It would really of course be the best for me to see it, but I don't suppose they will send it to me on approval. But I must do the best I can from your description. It is only a matter of your dropping in next time you happen to be in the West End. Make sure in any case that they reserve it.

Yes, I knew the "Scarlet Button" was being reprinted. I tried to get a copy within about three days of publication and it was already sold out. I wish they would do that with all my books.

I don't remember receiving the bills. If you would tell me what it was that you bought, I should be able to guess the price nearly enough.

That I think is all for this morning. It is quite possible that they may be able to fix me up next week so future letters had better be addressed to

> c/o Vernon Symonds, Esq.,
> Netherwood
> The Ridge
> Hastings, Sussex

> Yours etc.
>
> Aleister Crowley   pp. J.T.

P.S. Just had a telephone call - they may be able to fix me up in a much better way.

The complications which Crowley found too fearful to contemplate concerned his need for medicaments which he was taking against his severe bouts of asthma. His health was deteriorating rapidly and when I finally went to stay with him many of my services consisted in getting doctors and chemists to supply substances which they were far from eager to dispense. These included veronal, heroin, ethyl oxide, and cocaine. The state of Crowley's health necessitated such massive doses that one doctor in Hastings hinted to me in confidence that he feared that his patient was a drug addict! Nevertheless, despite his poor physical condition, Crowley never lost his mental elasticity and alertness.

Crowley is anxious for me to put a reservation on the mohur.

Netherwood,
The Ridge
Hastings, Sussex
February 7th, 1945

Care Frater,

Very many thanks for your registered letter with the Mohur, which I found {a}waiting me on my arrival. It is exactly what I wanted, and I must congratulate you most heartily on your success for it is a much better coin than the one which I nearly bought a year ago and for which they wanted £9.10. Talking of money, will it bother you very much to wait till after the 16th before I send it to you? The move was rather expensive, the car hire alone amounted to £15; and as I have not yet made any arrangements here about my board I do not want to leave myself absolutely flat, so if you don't mind waiting till my cable arrives you will make me very happy. The coin is just what I wanted, and your interpretation of it shows excellent Qabalistic thinking.

I have not yet had time to go into Hastings to ask about booksellers. In the meanwhile, a new scheme has entered the region of imagination. There is a cottage in the grounds here with two bedrooms, and (I gather) a kitchen and everything else that one wants, and it might be possible to arrange for us to occupy it. We could have meals in the house or as might otherwise be arranged. Now about finances: let me first explain that the owner of this place seems to have got into his head something very like the Abbey of Thelema which I started in Cefalù so many years ago. There is little or no service in the ordinary sense of the term; I have not yet got the hang of things but apparently everybody lends a hand when required more or less. Of course they are looking for regular help.

It has occurred to me that you might be willing to offer your services in return for board and lodging. You would give them so many hours a day, and keep an hour for working with me, and some time for yourself to work on your stenography and typing. There is no doubt a good school in Hastings; in fact, it is a comparatively civilised place. I have not broached the subject to the proprietor so far, as he is working with the Repertory Company here and does not get back till pretty late at night, and the lady of the house has been looking

Netherwood
The Ridge   May 5
Hastings
—

Dear Dr Clenmuck Smith

These unskilled people seem to be making
a regular habit of being two days late on a
Saturday.

I am so sorry to have to trouble you again, but
you would oblige me very much if you can spare
me 3 tubes of ⅙ gr (10 gr = ½ee)

I will send round in the course of the afternoon.

Yours sincerely,

Aleister Crowley

The supply of injection tablets should
have reached me on Friday. It did
not — nor Saturday either. (This
time the P.O. if any one is to blame;
the chemist telephoned that he had
posted it only the previous morning.

Now I cannot receive it before
Monday, + my reserves, probably owing
to the contrast — them — of 3 sleepless
nights, will be out by about 6 P.M. Saturday

So, as in similar circumstances
before, I hope you can let me have
10 gr.

— A. Crowley

[medical chart notes]

Caption: Medical notes.

after a sister who has been dangerously ill. (Very strange! she is the fourth person of my acquaintance within the last month who has had to go away to look after a sister dangerously ill). But I have a feeling that some sort of arrangement might be come to.

I don't think you ought to have any compunction. After all, if you went to a Guru in India, your first seven years would be solely devoted to delousing the Holy Man from time to time. I have also thought you ought to be able to induce your people or some of your wealthy aunts to grub-stake you in this gold mine.

Here are some suggestions for encouraging any such people. In the first place you would be carving out a career for yourself as opposed to an odd job. You will see of course that I could not get the O.T.O. to pay you a regular salary until you have fitted yourself completely for the post.

You would find a certain number of social or literary advantages in joining forces with me. You would meet people like Viscount Tredegar, Lady Aberconway, Lady Harris, Louis Marlow, Clifford Bax, and a number of other people, acquaintance with whom would be invaluable to you in the life of London.

In the second place, after my death you would become invaluable to the O.T.O., as being able to carry on with everything at the tips of your fingers, and I have no doubt that the Grand Treasurer of the O.T.O. would pay you a very good salary to look after the English side of the business.

Louis Marlow has accepted the position of my literary executor, and he will want an assistant. You would obviously be the man for the position; and for this work, too, you would be paid on a generous scale.

Please remember that so far this scheme is merely a wish-phantasm in my own disordered imagination, and it is really rather up to you to improve on it and materialise it.

Love is the law, love under will.

Fraternally 666

The first letter from 'Netherwood'.

The cable concerned the transfer of moneys which Crowley received regularly from his representative in America, the Grand Treasurer General of the O.T.O., Karl Germer. The sums consisted of gifts and subscriptions from members of the Order. For tax purposes, Crowley maintained that he subsisted on voluntary contributions; which, in fact, he did.

Germer was an eccentric, irascible German, who had transferred his allegiance from the German occultist Heinrich Traenker's Pansophia Lodge to Crowley's O.T.O. in the mid-twenties. Later imprisoned and exiled for his beliefs by the Nazis, he finally reached the U.S. in 1941.

On hearing of Crowley's final illness, he sailed for Antwerp on Friday 26th September 1947, but was refused entry to the U.K. They never met again.

Vernon Symonds, the proprietor of 'Netherwood', was an actor and a playwright who seemed to have had little success with his plays. His first gesture on my arrival at his guest-house was to present me with a printed and bound copy of one of them. He and his wife were a charming couple. They endeavoured to bring to Hastings in the grey days of the war something of the Bohemian verve we had known before it.

Crowley had sounded his treasurer, hence the drop in scale, from a salaried post for me with access to literary salons and aristocrats, to slopping about in the guest-house scullery and smuggling upstairs to Crowley more than his war-time ration of sugar. His idea of a cup of tea was a mountain of sweetness slightly dampened.

The sounding is contained in a letter which Crowley had written to Germer. I part-quote from my 'Netherwood' notebook a jotting from Crowley's dictation: "Grant: I dealt with this in the former part of this letter. What we must do is to organize: not only the Magick, but the literary side. This is a good moment to start some sort of society...We shall make definite plans after conference with people over here; and when they are cut and dried we shall present them to you to link up with U.S.A. 'fans' ".

The reference to "wealthy aunts" was prompted by an unwise allusion on my part to a relative in that category. After I left 'Netherwood', Crowley composed a bit of doggerel on the subject which I forbear to reproduce here.

Evan Morgan, Viscount Tredegar had a 'magic room' at Tredegar Park, Newport, Gwent.
Lady Harris was introduced to Crowley by the author Clifford Bax on Wednesday June 29th 1937. The Yî for that day was XLVII Khwan. Crowley's Yî for Frieda - cast on 9.5.38 - was XIII Thung Zan, "Union of Men".
Louis Marlow was the pen-name of Louis Umfraville Wilkinson, Crowley's life-long friend, and later one of his literary executors.

Netherwood   Feb 9 {1945}
The Ridge
Hastings   die ♄ i
Sussex   {Saturday}

C∴F∴
    93

Yours came this A.M. must have crossed mine, so thought needless to answer. But since then I have seen Vernon Symonds, and talked of you. I think he will jump with both feet, especially if you are content with little or no salary.
Being watery and Luna, the bulk of the help asked of you would be Washing-Up, the perfect preliminary Lustration in your initiation. V.S. did it himself for some months on

end, so I imagine it's tolerable; also, it would help you to realize that there are some who do nothing else from the first yell to the last rattle!

In any case, I suggest you take a day off – the best day is Friday, as V.S. doesn't have to go to the theatre – and come down. You could call on Brookes and Savile, the best booksellers here, and ask about the other scheme.

Train 9.45 A.M. Victoria

Back 5.5 P.M.

On arrival go to the Memorial & take a 'bus; they know Netherwood, so ask them to stop there. If week-day n.{o} g.{ood}, could you come as my guest next week-end? If so, tell me quickly, so as to be sure that I can book a room.

The cottage, seen from outside, should suit on a long-term plan. At present it isn't fixed up inside.

Let us think and act ιοζ ταχιστα, p.d.q. {pretty damn quick}. Should Orson Welles accept one of my plays next month, all financial doubts & difficulties will vanish in a flash.

Incidentally, the initiate, while avoiding imprudence, ought always to leave it to the Gods to do Their stuff. Such a habit leads to the successful performance of the "Act of Truth"; the mastery of which may one day be vital at a crucial moment.

93 $^{93}/_{93}$ Hoping to see you either 16th or 17-19th.,

Yours f∴ly 666.

Orson Welles became famous over-night for his updated version of H.G. Wells' *War of the Worlds*. When it was broadcast on American radio in October, 1938, it created widespread panic among listeners who supposed that Martians had invaded the Earth.

Crowley gives the formula of the 'Act of Truth' in the next letter.

G.K.Grant Esq
Netherwood
The Ridge
Hastings   Feb 13 {1945}

Care Frater,

   Do what thou wilt shall be the whole of the Law.

Glad to have yours of 11th. Unless we meet Colonel Pacton's brother, I should be able to hand you the doings on Friday or at the week-end: you don't say whether you can come, or, if so, on which day.

But now! Here I put on my mountain boots, and strap on extra tightly the steig-eisen, and jump, and jump, and jump.

"Steady pay". "Some source of steady income"! How many a tall ship have I seen wrecked on that abominable reef !

Woe's me!

There is no such thing, in this world, as security.

J.P. Morgan, who, the previous week had saved France from bankruptcy, was stopped at the French frontier for lack of cash to put up the deposit due on all cars entering France! He had to send a man back to the first big town while he kicked his heels at the douane.

I myself at the outbreak of the skirmish '14–'18 saw millionaires, dozens of them, all stranded in Berne without the price of a drink!

My poor innocent child, you don't seem to have the right idea at all about Magick.

You *must* take risks in any Magical Operation, if only because it is to insult the Gods (or the Masters) to hint that They may fail to do Their share of the Work.

There is a big case in California pending at this minute. A man went into an Ordeal, from which he was to emerge a God. He was to cut sharply across all old ties.

This is the sort of thing that might have happened. He picks out the first stranger, goes up to him, and says: "Good morning. Do what thou wilt shall be the whole of the Law. I am (? whatever God he had become). I have just come out of my Great Magical Retirement, and I propose to spend the first six weeks with you". *The Gods would have sent the right man to meet him.*

Instead – so far as I can make out from a cable received this morning – he is coming out as abject as he went in; no idea but to batten on his old associates as before.

Of course such an one must be prepared for charges of vagrancy, lunacy, or what not; that is all part of the game. But I believe that almost any man with a scrap of personality, could make a success of such an Opus – having a Banner to uphold. (He had one – claimed he was fanatically devoted to 93.)

Unless you can *believe* (Belief as that fire burns; i.e. you stake the success of your plans on the chance of its truth), you can never get more from Magick than the power to do various mild miracles; you will never attain to the Great Magick, which is identical with Life itself. Love is the law, love under will.   F∴ly 666.

The views which I had expressed about security were those of my anxious father, who later wrote to Crowley on the subject.

'Colonel Pacton's Brother' is the title of an approximately ten-thousand-words story by Crowley, written on a single day in August, 1920, at the Abbey of Thelema in Cefalù {see *The Magical Record of the Beast 666*}. A typescript of the story survives.

Crowley here identifies the Gods with the Masters – an interesting equation in view of the fact that at the time this letter was written a man named Wilfred T. Smith was undergoing, in California, a Magical Ordeal which could have transformed him into a Master – or a God. Crowley had presented Smith's case in a statement entitled *Liber Apotheosis vel 132*. 132 was the number of Smith's magical name or motto.

G.K. Grant Esq
Netherwood Feb 14 {1945}

C∴F∴
93
O.K. for ♄ {Saturday}
     arr{ive} Hastings 11.40.
Should try Brooke & Savile, best bookseller here, in Robertson St, 100 yds from Memorial, where you get Service 2 (Circular Route) 12.35 arr{ive} Netherwood (most conductors know it, or Ripon Lodge, or just past Sandrock) about 12.50 in time for lunch. Name of house in gate in big white lettering.
Disaster! Dropped this pen once too often; now I have to dip it, and even so - well you see! You seem to have the lucky touch: can you find me a new one? Prefer it a "presentation" specimen, with gold etc. Nib medium to broad if possible. Any old price! It's my life-line. Awkward writing at all with this; so I close.
93 $^{93}/_{93}$ F∴ly 666.

Crowley was soon to write a letter to the firm that supplied the pen in question. I quote the draft that survives in one of my 'Netherwood' notebooks:
Gentlemen,
I have a pen of yours which I bought something like twenty years ago in Paris. It is the kind in which you screw up the nib from the other end, so that it has to be filled from a dropper. The outside length is just $3^1/_2$ ", and the diameter of the cap just under half an inch. The pen is covered with a trellis-work of gold.
This pen has great sentimental value for me. The bag, or whatever it is in the cylinder, has been corrupted by time and then destroyed by some people who promised to put it right for me, so that it can only be used by dipping.
W.H. Smith and Son, here, promised to have it put right, and they returned it this afternoon saying their agents could do nothing. I should be extremely obliged if you could do something in the matter for me.
If you cannot repair it you might be able to let me have a new one of the same pattern, or if not some pen of exceptional...
{The remainder of the letter is missing}.

C∴F∴   Feb 21 {1945}
  93.
Am better, but it was a near thing this time!
Whatever happened to you? I could find only 1 page of the Corpse Story - stopped in mid-sentence (I've done the rest myself). Then Z.25 & Z.26 were to be taken to Miss

Taylor; but you left them! (I've sent them by post).

V.S. {Vernon Symonds} went sick too; so no news of Goulden or the rest. When I can move about the house, I will tackle the whole problem afresh. Probably I shall take the bit between my teeth, do a Light Cavalry operation, and fix all with a snap. So prepare for News!

93 $^{93}/_{93}$ Yrs fly {Yours fraternally} 666

PS.

N.B. Do get an exact figure for the amount of outside support. An uncertain figure is no figure.

––––––––––––

It might well be that we could arrange to start practically at once if I were able to guarantee to make up the deficit for say 3 months, even supposing you got no job at all. So you see why I *must* know how much I can depend on you for. 666

––––––––––––

At 93 Jermyn St - to be brought as early as possible. Collect any convenient occasion.

"Anglelight" Reading–lamp with jointed levers & red bell–shaped shade.

Tea cup & saucer & silver spoon.

Catullus - paper 8vo book in French & Latin: in shelves. 2 vols Rabelais trans by Urquhart and Motteux. Plain white pull–over, no arms or pockets. Smith's Classical Dictionary (black 8vo).

––––––––––––

Additional things I want from 93 Jermyn St.

––––––––––––

1. Head of Martinique boy with cigarette & coloured scarf. (chalks)
2. Head of girl smiling impudently ($^3/_4$ face) chalks.
3. Totem pole on pier, woman with bird behind. (Pen & ink)
4. The Great White Barrier of the Antarctic. (Water colour)
5. Self portrait of 666 vermilion background. (Water colour)

––––––––––––

6. Shaving mirror.
7. Big chessboard and men.

Z.25 and Z.26 denoted a system of classification pertaining to the series of letters for *Aleister Explains Everything* {*Magick Without Tears*}.

I took with me, to 'Netherwood', the articles required.

During my stay with him, Crowley suggested drawing up an inventory of certain items in his room {see Appendix 4}. The bookseller Michael Houghton was due to visit him a few days later; and Crowley said he had no wish to see his books - many of them rare first editions with holographic annotations - turning up on the second–hand market.

The inventory which I compiled mainly included objects visible to the eye. I had then no idea that the trunk which he kept under his bed was a veritable Pandora's box which probably contained the typescripts of the Cefalù and Paris diaries.

These were heart-rending human documents which I was to transcribe after his death, together with the later 'Royal Court' diaries. These copies now form part of the Yorke Collection of Crowleiana at the Warburg Institute.

At the time of my stay with him I knew nothing about his personal past. I had not read even the first two volumes of his *Confessions* {Mandrake Press 1929}. These – together with further unpublished material, which was in a parlous condition requiring months of editing and annotating – eventually appeared in print in 1969 {Cape}, 1979 {RKP} and 1989 {Arkana/Penguin}.

G.K. Grant Esq   Feb 22 {1945}

C∴F∴
   93
Dropped my pen twice more & now it's nearly right!
Haven't the courage to drop it on purpose!
Yours of 20th. Hope you have by now mine posted 8 A.M. 21st to 88, will have got data required, and have already answered it.
Urgent matter is your share of exes {expenses}.

—————————

Your – – – – week-end.
"I told you butter wouldn't agree with the works"
              Alice in Wonderland

—————————

Am much better; was wholly to blame for the attack. Still confined to room.
Perique came 21st.
Please send a Raphael's Ephemeris '34: don't let Atlantis know you know me.

—————————

One addition to Jermyn St bag; large portfolio of drawings.
Yes; please write to Aintree for that C.D.3. {Form concerning overseas mail.}
Thanks for doing odd jobs.
I think that's all.
93 $^{93}/_{93}$ F∴ly 666.
P.S. Keep in touch with J.T. {Janet Taylor}. She was promised a bottle of whisky early Feb by F & M {Fortnum & Mason}. She may want your help. A.C.

88 was the number of the house to which, until this date, Crowley's letters to me were addressed. I had just moved.

I cannot recall precisely the occasion which called for the quotation from Lewis Carroll; it may have been prompted by my efforts to extricate Crowley's

Contemporary photographs of Crowley and the author.

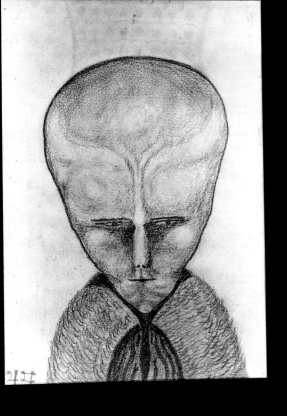

(left) The drawing of LAM mentioned in Crowley's letter of March 1945 (below), with dedication on reverse (facing page).

Ex nemore inferiori
Aretae Porti Novi

☉ in 29° ♓

Sol I xviii

Care Frater

Do what thou wilt shall be the whole of the Law

The drawing which you covet.

This drawing has a title. I do not mean an apt fancy, but a description accurate & recognisable by any person familiar with the subject, like "The Tower Bridge by Moonlight" or "Portrait of Mr Ernest Bevin" or "Burnham Beeches".

You are allowed 3 days and 3 guesses. If correct, the drawing is yours; if not, the test can be repeated at the Autumn Equinox

Love is the law, love under will

Fraternally 666.

To my very dear Foster Auwik 400 יהשוה 400
"a very present help in time of trouble" (Trouble = "Victory")
from T.B. Meya ⊕ppio 666
90 = 2° A∴A∴

The Bell Inn

Netherwood

93 Jermyn Street

belongings from the flat in Jermyn Street. His erstwhile landlady did not conceal her dislike of Crowley, and my attempts met with resistance. Crowley may have owed her money. However, I would like to place on record that as far as my own monetary dealings with him were concerned, he unfailingly honoured the debts which he incurred. But I do not think he ever understood that I was an impecunious youth at the time; and it never occurred to me to enlighten him.

On the table which he used for writing stood two large tins. One of them he had labelled with a large Hebrew letter ל , the other with the Hebrew letter פ . The former denoted Latakia, the latter, Perique, both strong and, need I add, expensive tobaccos. In a letter to Karl Germer {March, 1945}, he wrote: "Certainly put as much Perique as you can in store. It is now possible to get it in London, but I don't think the quality as good". On one or two occasions, I obtained it for him at Dunhill's.

'Raphael's Ephemeris', the well-known almanac containing astrological information.

'Atlantis', here, refers to the bookshop owned in those days by Michael Houghton.

Netherwood   Feb 25 {1945}

C∴F∴

{Scrawled beneath date}: I can't get V.S. {Vernon Symonds} to make up his mind about anything. A.C.

   93

Yours of 22nd & 23rd. Nothing much to answer, so I didn't.

Jermyn St: You may find trouble getting stuff cartable, esp{ecially} as I just recall that the miniature chest of drawers would be better here. If in trouble, apply COWTAN of Sloane Sq mentioning name of Mrs. Sutherland; they might help.

Bray {the binder of the *Book of Thoth*, at the firm of Sangorski & Sutcliffe}: Can't recall what particulars you want. Sorry.

———————————

Yours of 24th.

Glad you had no £15. "Michael" is the meanest thief alive. Even his fellow Jews - and you know how they hang together - spit on him for the foulness of his methods.

A good clean set {of *The Equinox*}, perfect, uniform, is worth £10. If with special attractions, such as notes by any one who counts, might fetch £12. A perfect "luxe" set {white & gold} say £15-20.

Do quench your boyish enthusiasms, & look at the world with the cold lack-lustre eye of the hard boiled business man!

C.D.3 seems as irrelevant as the rest. Will write more when well - still confined to room.

———————————

Agenda for Grant.

93 Jermyn St
Dale get knickles
Truslove & Hanson
F & M. } wine [see
H & B. }   over]
Atlantis Bookshop
Chocolate
The 48 letters
Pipe & Eastern suit,

Pipe: meerschaum &
amber (gold band) as
photographed in "The Fun of the
Fair".
To be packed in silk striped
Eastern dress & sent by post
registered.
—
All expenses (travel,
postage &c) to be charged
to A. Crowley.

Yes, one *should* include the 93 greetings whether "writing to my Lady or my butcher"; but it takes more courage than I have to do it all the time.
99 $^{93}/_{93}$ F∴ly 666
Will wire as soon as I can pin down V.S. {Vernon Symonds}.

Mrs. Sutherland: the wife of one of Crowley's chess cronies.

'93' Greetings, or Blessings: the quotation from *The Book of the Law* with which Crowley usually began and closed his letters. While at Hastings, he showed me an averse counterpart - a curse to be used on encountering members of the Christian and other 'old aeon' faiths. With a downward and outward sweep of the arm, and with eyes averted, one mutters *Apo pantos kakodaimonos* {"Depart from me all evil spirits"}. I did this one day when we passed two nuns on the sea front. Crowley halted, looked at me with mock astonishment, and said: "I wouldn't have had the nerve to do that".

Part of Crowley's love-hate relationship with the bookseller Michael Houghton, who often expressed similar feelings about him to me. As is well known, Crowley often let off steam by referring to his acquaintances in such terms.

Netherwood   Feb 28 {1945}

C∴F∴
    93
At last released from room! At last settled for you; never mind details. It's only for a month; gives you time to turn round; lets {sic} us start without further delay.

———————————

I enclose £5.5.0, not knowing how much (if any) "petty cash" J{anet} T{aylor} will have to hand to you.

———————————

Fortnum & Mason owe me a bottle of whisky since Feb 1; please make them cough up!

———————————

Get Mr. Upchurch of Hedges & Butler Regent St (REG: 4444). He promised me whisky - 4 bottles, I hope - for March 1. Please do your very damnedest to get him to produce them. "Royal Vat" is the kind I like best.

———————————

If you need more money, telegraph simply the amount required, and write confirming. Do keep some sort of a/c this time!

———————————

Please let me know as soon as possible what day to expect you.
Can't think of anything else at the moment.
93 $^{93}/_{93}$ F∴ly 666.

This clinches any controversy about Crowley's favourite brand of whisky. Fortnum & Mason, and Hedges & Butler, top Mayfair stores which supplied Crowley with drinks, which were in very short supply because of the war.

Netherwood   March 1 {1945}

C∴F∴
    93.

Those buckles have become most urgent. Two shops near top N. Bond St W side are likely. Antique silver is best. Price doesn't matter. Swaine & Adeney *might* have brass, or tell you where to go. They live Piccadilly just by Fortnum & Mason.
When got, shoot instantly to Mr. Dale 49 Chiltern St Baker St W.1.
He can't *start* shoes till he has them; so please make an extra push. If short of money, wire or telephone.
I can get out of doors now, IF fine, warm & windless. That means no hope for to-day!
Very busy wiping out arrears of correspondence
93 $^{93}/_{93}$ Fr∴ 666.

Netherwood   die ♀ - is
                                                             Friday
                                                             {Postmark 2 March, 1945}

C∴F∴
    93

It was on purpose that I gave you no details of the agreed terms.
It was natural of you to enquire; but even to allow yourself to wonder was magically wrong. Smack!

It is difficult to put the affair on an £.s.d. basis; but, roughly, your work is paid at about the same rate per hour as you are getting now. Then there are no deductions. There is no waste of time on journeys.
There is no foul London and Ilford atmosphere.
Your status is that of a guest, same as mine.
You are making yourself a career in the line you would have chosen had you been entirely free.
93 $^{93}/_{93}$ F∴ly 666

P.S. I forgot - please have Dunhill send $^1/_2$ lb Perique as before. Also $^1/_4$ lb pure Latakia.
I want this to reach me Monday A.M.
Best way might be to 'phone him to send it C.O.D.
A.C.

The first paragraph refers to the 'Act of Truth' {see Letter Feb. 13}, a vital tenet of Crowley's creed. From the stray remarks about it in this correspondence Crowley composed the letter later incorporated in *Magick Without Tears*.

Netherwood   March 4 {1945}
The Ridge
Hastings

C∴F∴
    93
Please forgive me for not answering: I had terrible news of a friend very dear to me, and I am still distressed.
However, work comes first. I want your help.
There seemed some hope of a printer, and I started to get OLLA into shape. To my surprise, I can find no examples to speak of of what was my longest & strongest suit – the rapture of Pure Beauty of Nature.
Will you buy for me, or sell or lend to me, my "Collected Works". If unavailable, Orpheus would have to do. If lent, you shall have it back as soon as I have the extracts I need typed out.
This may be urgent – I hope so. Please do your best for me.
What are your news? You would of course be most welcome here; any day would do. Room to be had outside if this joint is full.
93 $^{93}/_{93}$ F∴ly 666.
1 encl{osure}

Netherwood   die ☽ - ae
The Ridge   {Monday}
Hastings
C∴F∴
93
I suppose it is still a bit early to have news of your activities; still, you seem to have dug those buckles out of Dale!
Yesterday they made me lecture on Magick. Good crowd, & (by my standard) a success; for I managed to elicit a lot of really intelligent questions.
To-day I am planting Liber OZ on them.
Frightfully busy, clearing up the arrears.
93 $^{93}/_{93}$
All the best
F∴ly 666.

13. Please check up on the sequence of Al verses. You may miss a letter. If so I will have to re-fill the gap.

It is Easter and the House is crowded with frolicsome females & fanciful males. They got a hand down here & the Dame is in full swing. 666 would have this joke so we 'dressed up' and entered the Hall. He has a marvellous scarlet kimono (a present from Freeda) with long tassels appended to the sleeves). & he put this on & took His Wand. We waited in the dark outside until the Jazz stopped & then marched in. He gave the Greeting — I gave the Reply. They didn't quite know what to do; how to take it — but at last some really remarkable young lady came forward & said { "What is your will"
                              " " They will — it should have been

When we got back 666 said "This buggered me up properly!!" — she must have guessed!.

But the serious side to this Easter, on the exoteric planes — is this. Our mutual friend 'Michael' came down with Doreen (his wife). A rather unpleasant scene ensued upon his discovering my working down here. The 'servant' business didn't work, though I rushed about with a tray once or twice — to give the effect. Violet, the

Extract from author's letter to Steffi, from Netherwood.

The 'terrible news' is elucidated in a diary entry {March 4th}: "Dr. called unexpectedly; discussed optic Nerve of Horus. A little upset: I ask Message: IV Fang Thwan: don't be anxious. (Line 1 approves Alys)". This cryptic passage indicates that Crowley consulted the Yî King about severe anal discharges of blood that were causing him anxiety. The Eye of Horus, and 'Alys' - Crowley's feminine *persona* - show that in this instance he interpreted the Chinese oracle in a homosexual context: "The first line, undivided, shows its subject meeting with his mate. Though they are both of the same character, there will be no error. Advance will call forth approval" {Legge's translation}.

Olla, an Anthology of Sixty Years of Song. Crowley was selecting his favourite poems for this, his final production, which was printed in Hastings in 1946. It contains a portrait of Crowley drawn by Augustus John, and another on the dust-jacket by Lady Harris. It also included a poem entitled 'Thanatos Basileos', written at 'Netherwood'.

The poem 'Sekhet' {see illustration} appeared one morning on a scrap of paper left by Crowley on my table at the cottage in the grounds of 'Netherwood'. We had had an altercation the previous evening when he vainly expected me to present Thelema at an informal 'brain's trust' dreamed up by Vernon Symonds and chaired by Professor C.E.M. Joad, who had come down for the week-end. On a later occasion, Crowley did persuade me to socialize: I reproduce a fragment of my letter to Steffi dated Easter 1945.

Many interesting people used to visit 'Netherwood', and Crowley vainly tried to encourage me to meet them. I was entirely preoccupied with him, his work and his manuscripts stacked in his room, many of them then unpublished. I spent every spare moment copying them by hand, fearing they might be lost forever.

It is incredible how he managed to write his unique books -so perfectly produced - without a home, without reference books; wandering like a sadhu all his life from country to country, room to room, without any permanent base.

My preoccupation with his writings left me with with little time for - or interest in - anything else. So I hardly noticed such visitors as Frieda Harris or Dion Fortune. She had sent him a copy of her novel *Sea Priestess* in June 1944. On March 14th 1945 she had written to him: "The acknowledgement I made in the introduction to *The Mystical Qabalah* of my indebtedness to your work, which seemed to me no more than common literary honesty, has been used as a rod for my back by people who look on you as Antichrist. I am prepared to dig in my toes and stand up to trouble if I have got to, but I don't take on a fight if I can help it nowadays because it wastes too much time. I am fully aware that there *will* come a time when I shall have to come out into the open and say: this is the law of the New Aeon, but I want to pick my time for that, because I propose to be in a strong strategic position when I do so, and if you give Mrs. Grundy advance information, I may not be properly entrenched when the inevitable blitz starts.

Therefore I ask you not to mention my name for the present. I am at work on a book on the paths..."

On March 19th, 1946, Crowley wrote to Louis Wilkinson: "...Dion Fortune is dead. There was a very secret understanding, by which she acknowledged my authority..."

According to his diary, Crowley started preparing *Liber Oz* {see illustration} on October 10th 1941. He described it as "the O.T.O. Manifesto", and as a resumé of his "war-aims". It was published later that year as a single card, with a photograph of Crowley. Variations of the card included printings of the text on the reverse of Tarot trumps drawn by Frieda Harris, {see diary entries for Nov. 6th and 24th 1941}, and the version illustrated here.

March 5

C∴F∴
    93

Yours of 3rd.

O.K. Suppose you'll catch an evening train ♀ day {Friday} I got some brass buckles for Dale; now all I want is silver do {ditto} for breeches.

Miss M. {anning} is a curse; she thinks of nothing but her lousy spooks.

Upchurch of H & B {Hedges & Butler} is always very elusive. Best ask for him to have a parcel made up for you to pay for & collect.

This U.S.A. business is past all patience!

I'm quite O.K. but not going out in cold winds.

Did I mention emery boards for fingernails? Would like a packet or two.

93 $^{93}/_{93}$

In haste 666.

N. {Netherwood}   die ☿
                                                    {Wednesday}

C∴F∴
    93.

Fagged out dealing with U.S.A. mail!

Upchurch. Ask cost, and can he send by rail? If not, must put parcel aside for me to pick up when a chance comes.

F & M {Fortnum & Mason}. Better bring with you {i.e. whisky}.

Spencer. Since they can make, I'll get my own design, later.

Miss M{anning}. Always the same story.

93 $^{93}/_{93}$ F∴ly 666.

{on reverse}:

You don't say when you arrive here. Must tell them exact time.

666.

His erstwhile landlady was too absorbed in spiritist pursuits to help me to extricate Crowley's belongings, which she was holding, probably, against arrears of rent.

The shipment to America of *The Book of Thoth*. War-time restrictions baffled all attempts until I struck upon the notion of sending it through a City bookseller with whom I had had previous dealings. However, another source of agitation for Crowley was the "U.S.A. business" concerning the outcome of W.T. Smith's Magical Retirement, undertaken for the purpose of discovering his divinity, or otherwise. Crowley was writing acrimonious letters to Germer, and others, about Smith's "pernicious influence" {according to Crowley} over members of the O.T.O. in California. The rows culminated in Smith's expulsion from the Order, and Crowley's issuing an Interdict prohibiting members from communicating with Smith.

L.V. Upchurch; the man in charge at Hedges and Butler whom I had to persuade that Crowley was solvent. I succeeded, by dint of paying on the spot.

Netherwood

Kenneth Grant Esq.   {Postmarked 23 May, 1945}

die ☿ ii {Mercurii; i.e. Wednesday}

C∴F∴

   93

I was a little disappointed at not hearing from you this morning, if only your news.

(Please remember that this is the last week for those Personal Points: if no Choc{olate} cream, plain Chocolate; if not, barley sugar is always to be had.)

On Sunday they got me to lecture on Magick: a full audience, & from my point of view a great success; for I elicited intelligent questions. They too were surprised that I talked sound scientific sense instead of the expected

" fiddle sticks, blah, baloney

Bull-shit, and the Bunk "

I got rid of some Liber Al: they insisted on paying though I offered them free.

I wish you had been there.

———————————

No needles yet! I hope you are near Wigmore St., John Bell & Croyden (corner of Welbeck St) is pretty sure to have them. No. 20 $^1/_2$ inch

___

Terribly rushed; so - till later
93 $^{93}/_{93}$ F∴ly 666.

According to *Magick Without Tears* {Letter 15}, the couplet is attributable to Frances Ridley Havergal.

'20 Liber Al' refers to an American pocket-edition of *The Book of the Law* that had recently been published by the Church of Thelema, at 1003 South Orange Grove, Pasadena, California. {On one occasion, I went to the local post-office in Hastings to dispatch a cable to California. The official queried the address and asked me what state California was in! Crowley was delighted when I told him}.

Crowley was asking me to obtain needles for his hypodermic syringe. He was regularly injecting himself with heroin in accordance with his doctor's prescription.

Netherwood   {Postmarked: 25 May, 1945}
                                               die ♀ is
                                               {Day of Venus, i.e. Friday}

C∴F∴
   93
Very glad to hear from you: I was anxious.
Still more glad that you realize that "incompetence". Do please learn to be accurate! "*Some money for some postage*" means nothing. You must really make accounts
May 19th Postage to Ray Burlinghame n.p.

"	23rd	do	Mrs	do	n.p.
"	30th	do	Miss	do	n.p.

20th Bus fares &c	q.v.
20th 6 Needles	3.9.

and so on -
so that I can tell what has been done, & pay the exact sum required.
This is the first condition of our going to work together -which means lots of good Karma for you!
Miss K came up yesterday; we tried to straighten out the letters Mess. So far, there are some actually missing; G.O.K. {God Only Knows} how *that* happened. It is heart breaking; I can't do them all over again; it is never satisfactory.

___

Very happy to hear of your "gathering"; but the *first* thing is to get all those small commissions executed.

No answer from van Oppen; but a big parcel of Tarots came here from Bray {binder at Sangorski & Sutcliffe}; why? I didn't need any. Do get this all clear & the books on the way to ♄ {Saturnus = Karl Germer, in New York.}

You had no right to sign my private letter to Mrs. Felkin -not even p.p. or Secy! Wrong address, so it came back. What of that letter to J.W. Parsons? And do send me your notebook so that I can refer to originals.

93 $^{93}/_{93}$ In haste F∴ly 666.

Crowley dictated letters in two ways, depending upon the state of his health: like an express train, or through a muffling fog of phlegm. Both forms of delivery militated against the production of accurate texts, whether of letters or otherwise. If the faults were mine I can report a marked improvement over the past forty-five years, although when it comes to 'accounting', the incompetence remains.

Miss Kingston was the typist who supplanted Miss Taylor. Van Oppen was the name of the shipping agency through which Crowley sent books abroad.

Netherwood   May 30 {1945}

C∴F∴
    93

Yours with choc. cream duly to hand; Thanks: if you have one more set of points, please get them first week available.

Note-book: letter to J.W. Parsons not there. Can't understand.

All letters now found, sorted, put in order; I can now start going on with the series. One exception "Against asceticism"; perhaps this is there under another name.

All my fault anyhow.

Shall be very glad to hear of further activities - you've been a long while away, anyhow!

93 $^{93}/_{93}$ Yours in haste 666.

John W. Parsons was in charge of the Agapé Lodge in California, having taken over the post from Wilfred T. Smith whom Crowley had expelled from the Order. For an account of Parsons' strange history, and his involvement with L. Ron Hubbard, see *The Magical Revival* {Grant}, and *Bare-faced Messiah* {Russell}.

The Burlinghame family were members of Agapé Lodge.

One of my 'Netherwood' notebooks contained drafts of some of the letters dictated by Crowley, as well as various scraps in his own hand. One of these was intended for insertion in the letter entitled 'Sore Spots', published later in *Magick Without Tears* {see Appendix 5}. The 'motto' in French was to open the letter, and the remainder of the text was to have been inserted three paragraphs before the post-script.

The 'set of points' refers to the war-time food rationing system.

The Parsons letter was in another notebook.

"All letters", refers not to Crowley's day-to-day correspondence but to the collection of letters comprising *Magick Without Tears*.

Netherwood   June 1 {1945}
The Ridge
Hastings

C∴F∴
   93.
Yours of May 30 came this A.M.
Of course you are welcome - especially with the Visge! {Whisky} But you write as if you had actually bought it, & only needed to bring it. It's all wrong; you *must* learn to be systematic & accurate & unambiguous.

There used to be automatic machines (on piers & such places) with slots for pennies, and electrified handles. When you took hold you couldn't let go. How much more when you attach yourself in the most thorough & intimate way possible to a current like 93. It is good that you have now become a 'typhoid carrier' for the G∴W∴ {Great Work}.
But now that your sense of values is getting right, you ought to be clear that all your dodging & shuffling & funking won't work.
You must find a practice for Liber III which will not become automatic so easily. If, when I see you, you can show an arm with 50 or 60 honest cuts, I shall begin to have hopes of you. If the cut doesn't hurt, how are you to build up the sentry at the gate of your mind? *Do* quit that nonsense mock Qabalah. Why not A.{eon of} H.{orus} or A.{eon of} J.{esus} C.{hrist} or A.M. {?} instead of A.{nno} D.{omini}! There is no magical link between that conventional date and the names chosen for magical reasons.
93 $^{93}/_{93}$ F∴ly 666.

'Intimate' refers to anxious days and nights I had spent with him when he was too ill to be left on his own. The minutiae of daily war-time living were beginning to overwhelm him, and this was eventually reflected in the tone of some of his letters.

"Typhoid carrier": I was disseminating *Liber AL* and *Liber Oz* wherever I happened to be.

Liber III {see *Magick*, pp. 491-495}. It contains an exercise to induce alertness. One avoids a word or phrase that one would normally use frequently. Lapses in vigilance are registered instantly by a razor-nick on the forearm. See *The Equinox* I, iv, for a photograph of the arms of Victor Neuburg, one of Crowley's earlier chelas, who performed this exercise. It is not a practice I would recommend because the long term result is not control of thought and speech but, rather, a lessening of spontaneity and a dread of making mistakes. In other words, a substantial guilt-complex is engendered. In any case, why do violence to the body when the fault lies with the mind?

My 'mock' qabalah is perfectly legitimate. It is known in some circles as the 'theosophical' qabalah, the word theosophical being used in its etymological sense and having no connection with the Society of that name. Ouspensky alludes to the Theosophical Qabalah in connection with the 17th century mystic, Gichtel, author of the *Theosophia Practica*. The system has been widely used ever since.

I cannot now recall the reason for Crowley's strictures in the final sentence.

Netherwood   June 4 {1945}

C∴F∴
     93
Nothing from you this A.M. All you seem to have done is the sweets & the Note-book! Really!
The "48 letters" sent to ♄ {Germer} have been returned to me by the P.O. - why? Miss K. wrote to some H.Q. & got a letter back that you could send any parcel - no restriction on anything.
    So where are we?
    Needles. Nothing from Heppells or from you.
    Tried Chemists (opposite barber) they had plenty!
    Scarlet Button. First lending library I tried had a copy; they are reserving it for me when it comes in.
    Cowtan. I will send you (to Ilford) a note of the way I want you to get him to dispatch the various things.
I hope your holiday is doing you good, and that you will come back full of beans, and with your mind quite clear and your will set on getting these commissions executed.
93 $^{93}/_{93}$ F∴ly 666.
{Written on back of envelope:}
P.S. Library just rang up to say Scarlet Button came in this morning!

39

Heppells: the chemists, of Piccadilly.

Not being in London, I was unable to run around town on errands.

The '48 Letters': this refers to {for *Magick Without Tears*}

Netherwood   die ♄ i
                                                                    {Saturday}
C∴F∴   {Postmarked 16 June, 1945}
   93

Glad to get yours recd ♀ {Friday} & again this A.M.
Now is your chance to rehabilitate yourself – put all those jobs through *with a punch*.
McM. {McMurtry} just turned up!! Said you had written to him; that's a good mark.
He's here till ☿ or ♂ {Monday or Tuesday}; will deal with Mike when it's quieter.
All well here, but furious that I have no Uisge {Whisky} to give McM {McMurtry}.
Now then, on the job! And send me a regular report of what you've done, as soon as you've
done it. Your life hangs thereby!
93 $^{93}/_{93}$ F∴ly 666.

Liquor was in short supply towards the end of the war. Nevertheless, the stock at
'Netherwood' was by no means depleted and Crowley might easily have secured
a bottle of whisky from Mr. Richardson, the *major domo*.

Netherwood   June 21 {1945}

C∴F∴
   93

Thanks for yours recd ☿ [Wednesday]. But none this A.M. I asked you for a *daily* report.
All these trifles are *tests*, & you fail at every one. You *insisted* on having the Examination
paper. You make no attempt to answer it.

Jermyn St.
You say nothing of what you have fixed with Cowtan. You don't send Bertrand Russell's
Introduction to Mathematical Philosophy.
You were close both to F & M {Fortnum & Mason} & to H & B {Hedges & Butler} but
no word of the whisky.
It's all very unsatisfactory. You *must* put a sock in it, if you still want to work with me for
the Order.
93 $^{93}/_{93}$ F∴ 666.

The Examination Paper is reproduced in Appendix 1. It was set during my stay at 'Netherwood', and fell due at the Summer Solstice.

I was beginning to realize that Crowley's demands were unending. As Austin Spare frequently observed: "Enough is too much!"

> Netherwood
> The Ridge
> St. Leonard's-on-Sea
> 28.6.45

Care Frater,

    Do what thou wilt shall be the whole of the law. {sic}

At last I hear from you.

Will you please make a careful list of the clothes at Jermyn Street. You have not answered my question about Cowtan and I assume that you have done nothing. I have now written to them direct so you need not trouble any more about it.

I notice that although you actually passed Lechertier Barbe you have not troubled yourself to get the sealing wax, and you have not sent me the two pictures – the one of Katherine and the other of the same size for convenience of packing. You have also apparently done nothing about the Whiskey.

I have asked you for an explanation of your long-continued silence and neglect, and you did not say anything about it. Really if you are to continue in present relations you must attend to matters more punctually and fully. If you have been prevented by illness, why not write and say so.

Love is the law, love under will,

Yours fraternally,

pp. A. Crowley

{?} K. Sec{retary}

Lechertier Barbe: the colour-merchants' shop which then occupied premises on the ground floor, beneath Crowley's previous dwellings at 93 Jermyn Street. Crowley obtained there the wax with which he sealed most of his letters.

Cathrine* Falconer: A friend of Crowley who served in the Womens' Royal Naval Service. She paid occasional visits to 'Netherwood' during my stay there. He sketched her portrait in pastels. The picture survives. In a letter to Louis Wilkinson, Crowley wrote: "This is the Girl of Girls! You saw her impudently smiling face on my walls at 93 {Jermyn St.}. Now look for her; the other end is prehensile; God's greatest gift to any woman."

*Crowley's typist was in error.

Netherwood
The Ridge
St. Leonard's-on-Sea
9th July, 1945

Care Frater,

   Do what thou wilt shall be the whole of the law. {sic}

Thanks for your letter which arrived just in time to prevent me writing a stinker to your esteemed progenitor.

What you do not grasp is the purpose of my remarks. When I say I want a daily record of your activities on my behalf it is not because I am impatient or need them, it is because I am trying to get you into maintaining the discipline of the Order. It is natural for you to think 'Well, I did nothing yesterday; I have nothing to report, so I need not do it'. That is simply missing the point. I am trying you in half a dozen different ways, because the great fault that you have and one which will ultimately make it impossible for you even to pretend to carry out the great work is just that you cannot force yourself to be regular, punctual, accurate, and until you make it an absolute habit to exercise these virtues how do you think you are going to get on? {sic} when it is a question of pranayama or of work like the sacred magick of Abramelin?

Miss Kingston {the typist} suggests that The Heart of the Master has come back to you, like certain other parcels, because it was not properly packed, so far those sent by her have gone forward without difficulty.

The same remarks as above apply to this question of clothes. There should, for example, be a double-breasted black jacket with waistcoat and pin striped trousers, and there should be 2 silk waistcoats – a black and a white one. You do not give a proper list. Most of the things I cannot identify. You must learn to do things properly.

Of course Miss Manning does not care for you looking after my things, but she would prefer even that to taking on her own responsibilities. I wonder if her spirits have told her what is coming to her, but I cannot start to switch on the electrocution machine until I have an exact and accurate list of the clothes.

You really are a joke. You write "please excuse this speedy note but I will have to devote this afternoon to packing your copies of The Heart of the Master". Why should it take more than 5 minutes at the outside to pack 6 copies of a small book?

Love is the law, love under will,

Yours fraternally,

pp A. Crowley

M. K{ingston}

The letter which he eventually wrote to my father {see Appendix 6} was tinged, I thought, with nostalgia rather than with acrimony.

When Crowley died, two years later, a talisman 'for a great treasure' was found in his pocket-book. It was in the form of a magic square extracted from *The Book of the Sacred Magic of Abra-Melin the Mage.* For the Latin letters comprising the spell, Crowley had substituted Enochian characters. The talisman bore traces of the menstrual blood used in its consecration. I first saw it on a visit to Gerald Yorke in 1948. The book of Abramelin was the only volume in Crowley's possession which he seemed disinclined to let anyone see, much less handle. When we drew up the inventory previously mentioned, he merely indicated the locked drawer which contained it.

The Heart of the Master, originally published by the O.T.O. in London in 1938, contains meditations on the Ten Sephiroth and the Twenty-two Paths of the Tree of Life. A beautifully printed little book, bound in buckram and on handmade paper, it took only five weeks to produce - in those days. Sent to the printer on August 18th, the first proofs were ready 11 days later; the second proofs on September 5th, binding proofs on September 14th; advance copies arrived on September 22nd. It was published on September 23rd 1938!

Netherwood
The Ridge
Hastings   Aug 30 {1945}

Care Frater,
    Do what thou wilt shall be the whole of the Law.
It is some time since I heard from you. I hope that all is well with you.
Am I to consider you as still a Student of A∴A∴?
And what, generally, is the position?
Love is the law, love under will
Yours fraternally 666.

_____

Kenneth Grant Esq.   An Ixix ☉ in 0°0'0" ♎
                                                                          {Libra}
                                                          {i.e. Autumn Equinox, 1945}

De Castro
Nemoris Inferioris
    Do what thou wilt shall be the whole of the Law.
The Greetings of the Equinox of Autumn!
The Word of the Equinox is ROTARA.
The Oracle of the Equinox is Liber AL.II 22; with emphasis on the word "stir".
The Omen of the Equinox is Fâng 55.
Love is the law, love under will.
Your fraternally,
To Μεγα Θηριον 666
   9°=2□ A∴A∴

43

{On back of letter typed:}
The word is taken from the Abramelin square

```
S  E  A  R  A  H        { A variation of the Square 'for obtaining
E  L  L  O  P  A         Books of Magic' printed in the The Book
A  L  A  T  O  M         of the Sacred Magic of Abramelin the Mage,
R  O  T  A  R  A         Watkins, 1900}
A  P  I  R  A  K
H  A  M  A  K  S
```

Note that, spelt backwards, it is ARATOR, a sower or ploughman.
There is also obvious connexion with ROTA, TARO and cognate ideas. The emphasis is on the first A Venus in Taurus.

I had not submitted my Student's Examination Paper.

Crowley was, presumably, preparing his list of A∴A∴ members to whom he mailed twice a year the Word of the Equinox.

On the first days of Spring and Autumn it was Crowley's practice to 'send out' the Word of the Equinox. The Word, which none but a Magus can receive from the Secret Chiefs and transmit to members of the Order, epitomizes the Magical Current of the ensuing six months. In his earlier years, Crowley obtained the Word with the help of sexual magick. How he received it in his last years, I do not know. The Oracle, on the other hand, was obtained by opening at random the *Book of the Law*, and noting the word, or letters of a word, that came into contact with his seal-ring, the ring engraved with the cartouche of Ankh-af-na-Khonsu, a Theban priest of the XXVIth Dynasty, of whom Crowley claimed to have been a reincarnation. The ring was made for him by Max Schneider, an American member of the O.T.O. Many of the letters I received from Crowley arrived in envelopes bearing the impress of this ring {see illustration}. The Omen was derived from the Chinese Book of Changes {*Yî King*}. His method was to empty his mind and then to manipulate six flat pieces of tortoise-shell, approximately 1" by 5" in size. As the pieces fell they formed a figure, or hexagram, which Crowley then accepted as the Omen for the coming six months. As his diaries show, they were sometimes remarkably accurate.

22.1.46

Netherwood
The Ridge
HASTINGS

Care Frater,

Do what thou wilt shall be the whole of the Law.

You clamour for an answer to your letters, and when I write to you I get no reply.

Please tell me if you have done what I asked, and, is there any prospect of your coming to Hastings in the near future?

Love is the law, love under will.

Yours fraternally,

pp A. Crowley

M.K. {Kingston}

Netherwood
The Ridge
HASTINGS
15.3 46

Care Frater,

Do what thou wilt shall be the whole of the Law.

It was very kind of you to send me the books, but it so happened that a complete set reached me from another source by the same post, so that I did not have to open your parcel at all, and I am returning it.

As a token of good will however, let me renew my thanks.

With regard to Marriage. The Arabs have a saying that it is like a man who puts his hand into a bag with 999 poisonous snakes and one eel; he *may* pick out the eel.

I could add a great deal (if I had the time) on this subject, with which in connection with the past I have a good deal of knowledge and experience.

I should have thought The Secret Glory would have hindered you. But these impulses are really insane: ordinary rules do not apply. I wonder, however, if a prophetic strain was in you when you used the word 'furious'.

Love is the law, love under will.

Your ever,

Fly 666.

{In A.C's hand on folding Oz Card with photo. of A.C. in Arab costume.}

{postmark: 14 March 1946
Hastings}

Erratum

I was disturbed while reading over my letter. It should read: "Marriage, of which in connexion with the Path ..."

Sorry

666

45

Liber LXXVII

Oz:

"the law of
the strong:
this is our law
and the joy
of the world."
AL. II. 21

"Do what thou wilt shall be the whole of the law."
—*AL. I. 40.*

"thou hast no right but to do thy will. Do that, and no
other shall say nay."—*AL. I. 42-3.*

"Every man and every woman is a star."—*AL. I. 3.*

There is no god but man.

1. Man has the right to live by his own law—
    to live in the way that he wills to do:
    to work as he will:
    to play as he will:
    to rest as he will:
    to die when and how he will.

2. Man has the right to eat what he will:
    to drink what he will:
    to dwell where he will:
    to move as he will on the face of the earth.

3. Man has the right to think what he will:
    to speak what he will:
    to write what he will:
    to draw, paint, carve, etch, mould, build as he will:
    to dress as he will.

4. Man has the right to love as he will :—
    "take your fill and will of love as ye will,
    when, where, and with whom ye will."—*AL. I. 51.*

5. Man has the right to kill those who would thwart
    these rights.
    "the slaves shall serve."—*AL. II. 58.*

"Love is the law, love under will."—*AL. I. 57.*

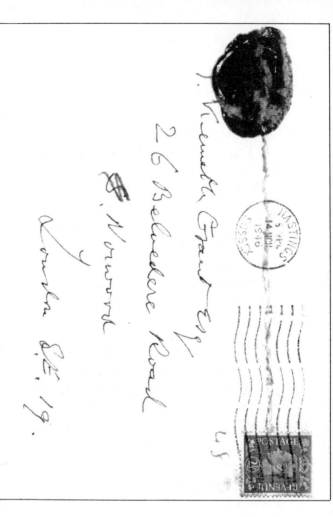

Two sides of Oz card folder.

The Erratum to this letter was on a folded sheet of hand-made paper displaying, on one side, *Liber Oz* {see illustration}, and on the other a photograph of Crowley in Arab costume.

I had committed the crime of getting married

Ex Castro
Nemoris Inferioris {Netherwood}

An Ixx ☉ in 0°0′ 0″ Aries
{Year 42 (of the Aeon of Horus)
Sun in Aries
(i.e. Spring Equinox, 1946)}

Care Frater,
    Do what thou wilt shall be the whole of the Law.
The Greetings of the Equinox of Spring!
The Word of the Equinox is SUHAL [1]
The Oracle of the Equinox is AL I 37 *the wand*
The Omen of the Equinox is Yî 42
Love is the law, love under will.
Yours fraternally
Το Μεγα Θηριον 666
9°=2□ A∴A∴
{In A.C's hand:}
[1] means a Black Lion; but is also a god or angel of generation.

P.S. Yrs {Yours} {i.e. acknowledgement of my letter to him.} Curwen knows 100 times as much as I do about Tantra. But I do not advise it.
Re IX° Be wary. If you do get the secret you have to be sworn in, or get into trouble with the Secret Chiefs. And that costs well over £100!
Found a printer!! Sending OLLA to press this P.M.
This, and sending out Words vide supra, keeps me *very* busy.
I very much want to see you. Couldn't you run down for lunch? Any day, bar Mondays.
666

Another 'Word of the Equinox'.

Crowley told me that the procedure was, that if I could tell him the secret of the Ninth Degree O.T.O., it would be his duty to confirm it, but only then. After which, I in turn would be required to take a special oath prior to admission to that degree. He suggested, therefore, that I write an essay setting forth my understanding of the matter. This I did, and he admitted that I had fathomed correctly the nature of the secret. It was an informal affair, as were most things where Crowley was concerned.

De Castro
Nemoris Inferioris   An Ixix ☉in0°0'0"♎

Care Frater,

Do what thou wilt shall be the whole of the Law.

The Greetings of the Equinox of Autumn!

The Word of the Equinox is ROTARA.

The Oracle of the Equinox is Liber AL.II 22; with emphasis on the word "stir."

The Omen of the Equinox is Fâng 55.

Love is the law, love under will.

Yours fraternally,

To Μέγα Θηρίον 666

9°=2□ A∴A∴

Ex Nemore Inferiori   An Ixix
Aretae de
Porto Novo   23rd. Mar. 1945 e.v.
☿▽⊥   die ♀.

Cara Soror Hyarim,

Do what thou wilt shall be the whole of the Law.

The Name of my Angel has this Day been accepted as such by Baphomet IX° O.T.O.

The Spelling is ר'חאיך

The Number is 400

Love is the law, love under will.

Fraternally
Fra.A. O.T.O.

Ex Nemore Inferiori   An Ixix
Aretae de
Porto Novo   ☉in 0°0'0'♈

Cara Soror Hyarim,

Do what thou wilt shall be the whole of the Law

The Greetings of the Equinox of Spring!

The Word of the Equinox is Άσταρτη

The Oracle is AL III 74 [Ring on (T)here is]

The Omen is 62. Hsias Kwo.

Love is the law, love under will.

Yours fraternally
Frater Assie
H. 666.

Ex Castro
Nemoris Inferioris   An Ixx ☉ in0°0'0"Aries

Care Frater,

Do what thou wilt shall be the whole of the Law.

The Greetings of the Equinox of Spring!

The Word of the Equinox is SUHAL*

The Oracle of the Equinox is

AL I 37   the wand

The Omen of the Equinox is Yū 42

Love is the law, love under will.

Yours fraternally,

To Μέγα Θηρίον 666

9°=2□ A∴A∴

* means Black Lion; but is also a golden angel of generation

Equinoctial Greetings, etc.

Not withstanding various disagreements, Crowley wrote in his diary after my departure from 'Netherwood': "Grant left, but arrangements very satisfactory for him to do my work in London". And in the 'Memo' section, he wrote: "Value of Grant: if I die or go to U.S.A., there must be a trained man to take care of English O.T.O.".

David Curwen was first mentioned in Crowley's diaries on 2.9.1944. When I met him, shortly before Crowley's death, he was a member of the IX° O.T.O. His passion for alchemy was all-consuming; so much so that he had nearly died after imbibing liquid gold. His knowledge of Tantra was considerable. It was through Curwen that I received, eventually, full initiation into a highly recondite formula of the tantric *vama marg*.

There exists a document relative to this formula compiled by Curwen's erstwhile guru, a South Indian tantric. It is in the form of an extensive commentary on an ancient text of the Kaula School. Curwen lent Crowley a copy of it. In it appeared an adverse criticism of Crowley's attempts at preparing the Elixir of Life. Against it, Crowley had scribbled: "He has not seen my ms. on the subject. But – no failure!"

But Crowley had not really succeeded, and it is not surprising. In the instructions which accompany the higher degrees of the O.T.O., there is no comprehensive account of the critical rôle of the *kalas*, or psycho-sexual emanations of the woman chosen for the magical rites.

The commentary was an eye-opener for Crowley, and it explained some of his preoccupations during my stay at 'Netherwood'. These involved a formula of rejuvenation. The O.T.O. lacked some vital keys to the real secret of magick which Crowley claimed to have incorporated into the higher degrees.

Curwen undoubtedly knew more about these matters than did Crowley, and Crowley was piqued. The *kalas*, or secretions of the tantric *suvasini* {the Scarlet Woman, as she is called in the Crowley mythos} became the subject of a typically Crowleian joke. He advised Curwen to call on a Captain Gerald Yorke who, Crowley said, retailed bottles of 'suvasini juice', much as he himself -in the days of *The Equinox* - had trafficked in Potted Sex-Appeal Ointment. Curwen followed the advice, and Yorke nearly died - laughing. Yorke told me later that this story, which I heard originally from Curwen, was true.

It is unfortunate that at the present time the full account of Curwen's involvement with Crowley cannot be related. I will just add that Curwen introduced Crowley to a lady known as Clanda, whom I had previously introduced to Curwen. She nearly became the third Mrs. Crowley. In a letter dated June 1946, Crowley drew up a list of aspects from her horoscope. Comparing affinities with his own, he exclaimed: "It is really an astonishing situation; it is as if you were my other half, or my daughter!" Clanda was the artist who drew the portraits of Steffi Grant included in this book.

Contemporary portraits: Steffi Grant, by Clanda; Kenneth Grant, by Steffi.

My own meeting with Curwen was brought about owing to his increasing suspicion that although he had been made a member of the Sovereign Sanctuary IX° O.T.O., the Order no longer existed, if it had ever existed, outside the pages of Crowley's books. Curwen therefore asked to be put in touch with some Order members, and Crowley gave him my name.

In a letter to Curwen dated 22nd January 1946, he wrote:

"By the way it might interest you to meet some of the very young generation. I should perhaps have mentioned the man in my previous letter, but I was overworked and nervous. The name is G. Kenneth Grant. I believe he works for a bookseller in the City and it should therefore be easy for you to arrange to lunch together. He is a very strange though decidely interesting man, and I should very much value your opinion of him. Do you think in particular that he can ever develop into a responsible leader. He was down here for some weeks with me, but under rather trying conditions for him and I feel that I may have treated him too severely."

APPENDIX I

Students' Examination

An Ixix ☉ ☌ ☿ in 21° ♉ {April, 1945}

_____

1. Buddhism may be divided into these classes:
    1 Hinayana (Burma, Siam, Ceylon)
    2 Mahayana (Tibet)
    3 Twelve sects in Japan
    4 Chinese Buddhism
What divisions of Christianity correspond to each, and why?

_____

2. What is the meaning, & why, of the following numbers:
    148.
    210.
    831.
Reconcile the two apparently conflicting series of meanings of the number 65.
Work out the equation $3 = 4$ especially in relation to the Sephiroth and the Planets.

3. State the difference between Vedantism, Sufism, & Molinism. Can you trace any historical sequence in these branches of Mysticism?

4. A friend's cows suffer from some epidemic disease. How would you set to work to discover the cause; if due to bewitchment, how to detect the agent; and how would you proceed to avert the evil?

5. Describe a woman with ♅ ☌ ☿ △ ♀ rising in 8° {?} ♑ .

_____

The answers to these questions are to be submitted on An Ixix ☉ ☍ ☾ in ♊ 6°

666   {1945}

The examination was eventually passed and I was exhorted, almost immediately, to begin the tasks of a neophyte. This surprised me, as the usual procedure required a year's probation.

1. Buddhism may be divided into these classes:
1. Hinayana (Burma, Siam, Ceylon)
2. Mahayana (Tibet.)
3. Twelve sects in Japan.
4. Zen (Japan)
5. Chinese Buddhism.

What divisions of Christianity correspond to each, and why?

2. What is the meaning, & why, of the following numbers:
148.
210.
831.

Reconcile the two apparently conflicting series of meanings of the number 65.

(pt/)

Work out the equation 3 = 4 especially in relation to the Sephiroth and the Planets.

3. State the differences between Voodooism, Sufism, & Yohinism. Can you trace any historical sequence in these hierarchies of Mysticism?

4. A friend's course suffers from some stridenic disease. How would you set to work to discover the cause; if one to hurt/detect the agent; and how would you proceed to meet the bad? Describe a ... using ... 0.73.

5. The answers to these questions are to be submitted on A I xix ⊙ ♂ (in II 6°

666.

APPENDIX II

{see letter dated February 21st., 1945}.
Inventory of Books in possession of A.C. at the time of the above letter.

Formal Logic, by J. Nevill-Keynes
The Equinox (boards) (Crowley & others)
The Equinox (two numbers bound in white buckram)
Discourse on the Worship of Priapus by Richard Payne Knight (original edition)
Copies of *The International*, bound up. (With articles by A.C.)
Typescript of Short Stories.(Crowley)
1001 Nativities
The Book of Lies (Crowley)
The Stratagem (Crowley)
Book Four, Part I (Crowley)
The Heart of the Master (Crowley; special edition)
Nuttal's Dictionary (black cloth)
Skeat's Etymological Dictionary (red cloth)
Les Fleurs du Mal (Baudelaire) (black morocco)
Two envelopes containing typescripts of translations of same.
Little Poems in Prose (Bandelaire)(Eng, trans. A.C.; original edition)
Photograph of *The Book of the Law* (No. 6 of 11 copies)
The Legend of Aleister Crowley (Stephensen)
Browning's Collected Works (2 vols)
The Lonely Ones (Steig)
The Diary of a Drug Fiend (copy with key)
Another copy with original contract offer to Collins.
Bab Ballads by W.S. Gilbert
Liber 777 (A.C. & others: private copy)
Konx Om Pax (A.C.) (Crimson & gold morocco binding; Japanese vellum) (1 of 10 copies).
The Winged Beetle (A.C.)
Mortadello (A.C., private copy; original poem facing title page).
Olla typescripts
Smaller Classical Dictionary (Oxford)
Temperance: A Tract of the Times (A.C.) (Ed. copy)
The City of God (A.C.) (Ed. copy)
The Fun of the Fair (A.C.) (Ed. copy)
Liber II (American Ed.)
Thumbs Up! (A.C.) (American Ed.)
The Fun of the Fair (No.0)
The City of God (No.0)
Tao Teh King (Typescript bound in grey cloth).
Why Jesus Wept (Crowley) (Bound in violet paper).
Liber LXV (Crowley; blue cloth).

Eight Lectures on Yoga (Crowley).

Thumbs Up! (Crowley: special copy with comments).

La Gauloise (Crowley: inserted in *Thumbs Up!*).

Temperance: A Tract of the Times (Crowley: unnumbered copy)

The Equinox of the Gods (Crowley) (Special copy with press cuttings).

The Hag (i.e. *The Confessions of Aleister Crowley*). Vol.II.

The Book of Thoth (Crowley: key copy).

Magick in Theory and Practice (Crowley: special copy prepared for enlarged edition).

Rabelais (2 vols: pub. Lawrence and Buller).

Musée de Naples (Harris, 1857).

In left-hand top drawer of chest-of-drawers:

Ms. of The World's Tragedy

Book of Abramelin Squares.

Original Ms. of *The Book of the Law*.

Behind *Stélé of Revealing* (copy on wood) on chest-of-drawers:

Khing Khang Khing (bound in old paisley broidered stuff).

On shelf by wash-stand basin:

Vols. IV VI, inclusive, of *The Hag*. (in typescript).

The Book of Thoth :(2 copies).

In trunk beneath bed list not made, but of several items I recall:

Typescript of extended commentary on *The Book of the Law*, in 3 springback binders.

My Life in a Love Cult: My True Life Story by Marian Dockerill. (pub. Better Publishing Company, Dunellen N.J.) Chapter 9 contains a sensational account of Crowley and the O.T.O. {see illustrations}. Crowley handed it to me with a smile: "You may find this rubbish enlightening". But he had carried this "rubbish" around with him for nearly twenty years, such was his delight in being vilified by his traducers.

Marian Dockerill was a sister of Leah Hirsig, Crowley's chief Scarlet Woman during his Cefalù period.

could have understood it happening to me, even though Aleister Crowley, the infamous "Beast," repelled me. I had come to know how close the shade between repulsion and love.

But Lea!

My voice was a husky whisper. "Has—has this gone—far?" I asked.

She pulled herself up proudly before me, like a queen, and threw aside the crimson robe that only partially concealed the once virginal white body I had known.

She Is Branded

There, branded deeply on the snow-white of her skin, was a great star inside a double circle. The anger of the outraged white flesh flamed redly at me. My sister swayed and spoke dreamily.

"I—I am his High Priestess! I am his 'Woman of Babylon!' Not the scarlet woman of the putrid-minded, but the scarlet maiden of the Apocalypse, forever bound to him by this, to him, my Beast, my lover, my Anti-Christ! Here—right here," and her arm dramatically described an arc toward the center of the studio floor on which I could see a faint chalk-line circle, "is where he made me his own. Inside this circle I knelt, adoring him. With his own dagger, white-hot, he branded me his chattel forever! Ah, the exquisite agony! The joy!"

Had Taken Her Body

It was true, too horribly true. That devil-man had, in a night, taken her body. Had he, too, taken her mind? She swayed, about to fall. I sprang toward her.

I was too late. The curtains were flung violently aside. The beast-eyed Crowley leaped across the studio. It was into his outstretched arms she fell. He laid her on a couch and stood over her glaring his defiance at me.

I hate, even now, to glimpse in retrospect the scene that followed. Never before, never since, had or have I been so beside myself. I raged, I tore, I threatened, I pleaded, I cajoled. All to no avail. They laughed at my tears. In their love-crazed condition, all arguments were useless.

To Aid My Sister

I realized at length, as my passion wore itself out, that, if I were really to aid my sister, to bring her back to sanity, I must try to remain on as good terms as possible with Crowley. I did my best to get a grip on myself. That was my idea throughout the luncheon I had with them, and at which appeared another masculine devotee of Crowley's Great God Pan.

When I left them, "The Beast" was seated at a table,

absorbed in a game of chess with a boon companion. At his feet lay my sister, sound asleep, completely nude, curled up in cushions like a drowsing kitten.

Poor little "goddess!" Neither "The Beast" nor his companion paid the slightest heed to her who had been dubbed "Goddess" and "High Priestess," but who seemed, now, more like a pet animal or docile slave.

The Transformation

I had been the unwelcome witness of one of the "miracles" Crowley boasted he could, with the help of his Satan, perform. For that twenty-four-hour transformation of my innocent little sister was the strangest thing I have ever witnessed—a miracle, truly diabolic!

The most striking thing about that man was his belief in himself, that he was an actual devil-god. The burden of his chant, that which he taught his followers was: "Love is the law. Love under will."

I think in that neurotic mind of his he really believed he was going to raise humanity to a higher plane, but he certainly went about it in a most peculiar way.

The Right of Wrong

Once, when I attended one of his public lectures, I saw how his teachings were received by people of normal minds. So wild were his ideas, so warped, that the hall which had been reasonably well filled, was more than half empty before he had concluded.

He believed that whatever anyone wanted to do was right, regardless of whom he injured.

You may think there was scant difference between this teaching of his which I condemn and my own ideas of following impulse, defying convention.

There was this great difference: Crowley believed in the "right of wrong." To him the worshiping and following of Satan and evil were the highest to which one could attain. His idea was: "All is evil. Evil is right. Let evil prevail!"

All Is Good

And I? My belief is that "all is good, for all is God." There is no right or wrong in the Universal Plan, but there is free will to follow impulses and, what is more important still, to control them.

The difference between Crowley's freedom and mine is the difference between following impulse in the belief of its right, in mind and motive, defying convention because of honest belief, and the following of evil for evil's sake, defying all for the sake of defiance.

It would never occur to me to say that anyone could successfully defy the laws of Nature. Aleister Crowley

MY LIFE *in a*
LOVE CULT
A Warning to All Young Girls

*Marian
Dockerill
at the age
of 54. Still
beautiful
and loved*

My True Life Story *By*
MARIAN DOCKERILL
High Priestess of Oom

Published by the
BETTER PUBLISHING COMPANY
DUNELLEN, N. J.

APPENDIX III

Ex nemore inferiori {Netherwood}
Aretae Porti Novi {Hastings}   An I xviii {sic} {1945}
                                                        ☉ in 29° ♓ {February 15th}

Care Frater,

  Do what thou wilt shall be the whole of the Law.

The drawing which you covet.

———————————

This drawing has a title. I do not mean an apt fancy, but a description accurate &
recognisable by any person familiar with the subject, like "The Tower Bridge by Moonlight"
or "Portrait of Mr. Ernest Bevin" or "Barnham Beeches".
You are allowed 3 days and 3 guesses. If correct, the
drawing is yours; if not; the test can be repeated at the Autumn Equinox.
Love is the law, love under will.
Fraternally 666

———————————

{The reply to my effort.}
I thought I had explained carefully that I wanted an answer, not a sermon! If I point to a
tea-pot, and ask "What is that?" You don't say "The refreshing beverage which we owe
to the Chinese calms the mind, and induces a state of feeling which is conducive to carrying
on one's work" etc., etc.
This is a terrible defect in your outlook on life; you cannot be content with the simplicity
of reality and fact; you have to go off into a pipe-dream.
Yet you wouldn't do this with the other pictures on the walls; you would say rightly "a
girl's head" or "Boy from Martinique" or "Snow-peak beyond foothills" & so on, as the
case may be. Idealism is the way to Falsehood. 666.

Crowley was being difficult. My description was concise, considering that at that
time I had not seen the portrait of Lam reproduced in the Blue Equinox in 1919.
Crowley reconsidered his assessment and, a few days later, he handed me the
picture with a dorsal inscription {see illustration}. He had suffered grave bouts
of asthma, and on May 8, 1945, he wrote in his diary: "Aussik helped a whole
lot; gave him 'The Lama' ". Crowley told me that the portrait had been drawn
from life. This was long before public awareness of UFOs or ETs. That Lam is
a link with the Company of the Outer Ones to which Aiwass belongs, did not
become apparent until the Workings of New Isis Lodge in the mid-fifties.
Looking back now with an awareness of the numberless individuals with whom

Wax seals, with imprint of Ankh-af-na-Khonsu ring.

Crowley's Masonic headdress and medallion, his copper dagger; and two G∴D∴ sashes.

Crowley had had contact – for he was curiously mercurial for one engrossed in occult pursuits – I am astonished by his patience. He was always prepared to give me his complete attention when it came to matters of magical instruction; *and* he was prepared to listen as well as to explain.

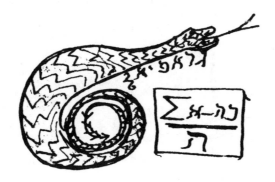

The sigil of Graphiel, Intelligence of Mars.

400. You forgot to bring me envelopes.

Do you ever miss an adoration?

Do you always remember to say Will & meal?

Are you learning one chapter of Liber AL by heart?

Are you doing any Yoga practices?

Why did you forget Rehearsal 3rd Paw?

Do you know the ☆ ritual by heart? And perform it at least twice a day?

Will you remember that a number is composed of its factors, if any? (You have no right to neglect the ×10 or ×100, or ×1000, etc ∴ .6645 = 1 × 3 × 5 × 7 × 9; not 6+6+1+5 = 18.) One makes constructive sense; the other is a jumble.

What progress have you made with your Magical Record?

Frater 400

93.

Part of Neophyte Task is to choose a chapter of Liber LXV & commit it to memory. Do this at once!

93 93/93

Fiat 666

APPENDIX IV

> You forgot to bring me
> envelopes.

400

Do you ever miss an adoration?

Do you always remember to say Will/meal?

Are you learning one chapter of Liber AL by heart?

Are you doing any Yoga practices?

Why did you forget The Great God Pan?

Do you know the ☆ ritual by heart? And perform it at least twice a day?

Will you remember that a number is composed of its factors, if any? (You have no right to neglect the x 10 or x 100 or x 1000, etc. 6615 = 1 x 3 x 5 x 7 x 9; *not* 6 + 6 + 1 + 5 = 18.) One makes constructive sense; the other is a jumble.

———————

Frater 400

93.

Part of Neophyte Task is to choose a chapter of Liber LXV & commit it to memory. Do this at once!

93 $^{93}/_{93}$ F∴ly 666.

Please call soon.

A.C.

The number 400 was that of my magical name, Aossic, which Crowley in his diaries spelled in a variety of ways, such as OShIK, A'AShIK, OSSIK, A'ASIK, AUSSIK and AOTzK.

The 'adoration' refers to the daily practice of *Liber Resh vel Helios* in which the aspirant greets the sun at its rising, setting, zenith and nadir. The purpose of the performance is to attune the magician to the Solar-Phallic Energy that informs the Magical Current associated with Aiwass {93}. It also keeps the adorant mindful of the Great Work, i.e. the use of the current to merge individual into universal Consciousness. {For *Liber Resh*, see *Magick*, Arkana, p. 489-490}.

I shall always remember entering Crowley's room one morning; he was strolling in the grounds of 'Netherwood'. The paunchy, seedy, bohemian appearance of a decade ago had given way to a refinement that suggested the fragile ivory figure of a mandarin, of which the hands were, perhaps, the most singular feature; slightly yellow, beautifully articulated and curiously small. Approaching the house, he threw up his arms and muttered the lines from *Liber Resh*: "Hail unto thee who art Ahathor in thy beauty" - the midday adoration.

Will/Meal: At meal-times the aspirant says 'Will' as a Christian says 'Grace', that the physical substance {food and drink} which he consumes might be transmuted into spiritual substance or Light, for the purpose of Enlightenment, or achieving the Great Work.

The Great God Pan: One morning at 'Netherwood', when Crowley accompanied me from the guest-house to the cottage, we experienced a joint 'vision' of a satyr-like form in the early spring sunshine. This could have been the result of an invocation Crowley and I performed in the grounds of the cottage where I was staying. I had left the front door ajar whilst going to fetch Crowley from the guest house. He would often come over to the cottage - weather permitting - and dictate a few letters or chat about magick.

On that particular morning I could see that he had other intentions. In a tremulous falsetto voice he began intoning the chorus to his "Hymn to Pan", and I joined in. By the time we reached the cottage, the chant had acquired an hypnotic intensity. Inside, I opened a window which flashed a shaft of sunlight onto a dense bed of ivy leaves. A thin haze hung over the ground. The brilliant, glancing light revealed an almost human countenance wreathed in foliage. It was not entirely a figment of my imagination, for Crowley also saw it. The incident loses in the telling - such experiences are virtually incommunicable - but the impression remains today as vivid as it was forty-five years ago.

He is chiding me with having omitted a daily ritual which he devised for me in order to maintain communication with the entity we had seen; a reflex of Pan.

The Star signifies the Pentagram. A reference to the 'Lesser Ritual of the Pentagram' which the magician performs daily. See *Magick*, Arkana, pp. 451-453.

Liber LXV is *Liber Cordis Cincti Serpente*, *The Book of the Heart Girt With the Serpent*. It treats of the relationship between the Magician and his True Will {Thelema/93}, embodied as a *daemon* or *angel* for purposes of magical and/or mystical intercourse. {See *The Equinox*, III.I.}

The glyph {see illustration} was drawn by Crowley on an envelope which he left on my table at the cottage, with instructions to investigate the nature of the entity depicted, and its potential as an astral guide. The curious creature represents the Intelligence of the planet Mars. The sum of the series of numbers, denoted by the Hebrew letters, is 325, which is the number of GRAPhIAL {Graphiel}, the name of the Intelligence in question.

APPENDIX V

Motto for
> "Sore Spots"

_____

"Il n'appartient vraiment qu'aux races dégradées
D'avoir lâchement peur des faits et des idées."

"Appelez bien plûtot sur ce qui vous effraie
Le jour qui rétablit la proportion vraie,
Et dépouille l'objet, à lui-même réduit,
De l'aspect colossal que lui prêtait la nuit."

Ponsard. *Charlotte Corday*. Prologue.

Insert in "Sore Spots"

Here is a case in point from recent experience. In my play "The Three Wishes" one of the characters is a rich selfish woman who has exhausted every source of vicious pleasure. In her abject despair her last resource is addiction to morphine.

I gave the play to an actor, a man of the highest intelligence and the broadest views on life; he said that I could not hope to get a play licensed if it dealt with drugs, unless as a warning against their abuse - which is exactly what the play imports. The mere mention of morphine had so disturbed his judgement that he failed to realize that fact.

He interpreted her abject wail, the cynical cry of a damned soul, as a defiant assertion of compensation for her disappointments in all else.

The mere mention! There is not a line in the whole play to support any advocacy or excuse for her suicidal habit.

This insert was intended for the letter, "Sore Spots", in Magick Without Tears. It has languished until now in one of the 'Netherwood Notebooks'. I include it here for the benefit of those who may wish to add it to their own copy of the book.

APPENDIX VI

{A letter to my father}

Netherwood
The Ridge
Hastings   May 14 {1945}
G. Grant Esq.

Dear Mr. Grant

Do what thou wilt shall be the whole of the Law.

Many thanks for your letter of the 12th inst with enclosure cheque £6.0.0.

I am very sorry to part with Kenneth, as I had agreed to consent to your terms for a month, which would have given me time to get consent from my Treasurer in New York to make it permanent – and I must confess to some annoyance at being abandoned, with everything in confusion, at 24 hours' notice.

I feel moreover that he is giving up his real future. I have found it impossible to get him interested in anything but the very highly specialized work which occupies most of my time, and I am afraid that he will never devote himself to advancement in any other career, which is of course the first condition of success. On the other hand, his real abilities which are great will be totally wasted.

Love is the law, love under will.

Yours sincerely

Aleister Crowley

TITLES BY ALEISTER CROWLEY

Edited, annotated and introduced by his literary executor John Symonds, and by Kenneth Grant.

COMPLETE ASTROLOGICAL WRITINGS THE. Duckworth 1974.
Contains *A Treatise on Astrology, Liber DXXXVII* from *The Equinox I.10, 1913,* and an article from *The International* 1917.

CONFESSIONS OF ALEISTER CROWLEY THE. Cape 1969. RKP 1979. Arkana/Penguin 1989. {Part published 1929}.

DIARY OF A DRUG FIEND THE. Sphere 1972. {First published 1922}.

HEART OF THE MASTER THE. 93 Publishing 1973. {First published 1938}

MAGICAL AND PHILOSOPHICAL COMMENTARIES ON THE BOOK OF THE LAW. With reproduction of the original manuscript of *Liber AL*, and the Djeridensis Working {'the Comment called D'}. 93 Publishing 1974.

MAGICAL RECORD OF THE BEAST 666 THE. Duckworth 1972. Also contains *Liber AL*, with the 'short' Comment.

MAGICK. RKP 1973 Arkana/Penguin 1989
Contains *Book Four Part I* {First published 1913}
Book Four Part II {First published 1913}
Book Four Part III: Magick in Theory and Practice {First published 1929}

MOONCHILD. Sphere 1972 {First published 1929}

TITLES BY KENNETH GRANT

*THE MAGICAL REVIVAL. Skoob Books Publishing Ltd., 1991
{First published by Muller 1972}

*ALEISTER CROWLEY AND THE HIDDEN GOD. Muller 1973

*CULTS OF THE SHADOW. Muller 1975

IMAGES AND ORACLES OF AUSTIN OSMAN SPARE. Muller 1975

*NIGHTSIDE OF EDEN. Muller 1977

*OUTSIDE THE CIRCLES OF TIME. Muller 1980

HIDDEN LORE. {With Steffi Grant} Skoob Books 1989
{First published in ten parts as THE CARFAX MONOGRAPHS 1959-63}

Skoob Books Publishing will be reprinting the asterisked books from the Trilogies in chronological order, and will shortly be publishing the book that completes the second trilogy; HECATE'S FOUNTAIN.